Semantics Empowered Web 3.0

Managing Enterprise, Social, Sensor, and Cloud-based Data
and Services for Advanced Applications

Synthesis Lectures on Data Management

Editor
M. Tamer Özsu, *University of Waterloo*

Synthesis Lectures on Data Management is edited by Tamer Özsu of the University of Waterloo. The series will publish 50- to 125-page publications on topics pertaining to data management. The scope will largely follow the purview of premier information and computer science conferences, such as ACM SIGMOD, VLDB, ICDE, PODS, ICDT, and ACM KDD. Potential topics include, but not are limited to: query languages, database system architectures, transaction management, data warehousing, XML and databases, data stream systems, wide scale data distribution, multimedia data management, data mining, and related subjects.

Semantics Empowered Web 3.0: Managing Enterprise, Social, Sensor, and Cloud-based Data and Services for Advanced Applications
Amit Sheth and Krishnaprasad Thirunarayan
2013

Foundations of Data Quality Management
Wenfei Fan and Floris Geerts
2012

Incomplete Data and Data Dependencies in Relational Databases
Sergio Greco, Cristian Molinaro, and Francesca Spezzano
2012

Business Processes: A Database Perspective
Daniel Deutch and Tova Milo
2012

Data Protection from Insider Threats
Elisa Bertino
2012

Deep Web Query Interface Understanding and Integration
Eduard C. Dragut, Weiyi Meng, and Clement T. Yu
2012

Privacy-Preserving Data Publishing: An Overview
Raymond Chi-Wing Wong and Ada Wai-Chee Fu
2010

Keyword Search in Databases
Jeffrey Xu Yu, Lu Qin, and Lijun Chang
2009

Semantics Empowered Web 3.0: Managing Enterprise, Social, Sensor, and Cloud Based Data and Services for Advanced Applications

Amit Sheth and Krishnaprasad Thirunarayan

www.morganclaypool.com

ISBN: 9781608457168   paperback
ISBN: 9781608457175   ebook

DOI 10.2200/S00455ED1V01Y201211DTM031

A Publication in the Morgan & Claypool Publishers series
SYNTHESIS LECTURES ON DATA MANAGEMENT

Lecture #31
Series Editor: M. Tamer Özsu, *University of Waterloo*
Series ISSN
Synthesis Lectures on Data Management
Print 2153-5418   Electronic 2153-5426

Semantics Empowered Web 3.0

Managing Enterprise, Social, Sensor, and Cloud-based Data and Services for Advanced Applications

Amit Sheth and Krishnaprasad Thirunarayan

Kno.e.sis Center, Wright State University

SYNTHESIS LECTURES ON DATA MANAGEMENT #31

ABSTRACT

After the traditional document-centric Web 1.0 and user-generated content focused Web 2.0, Web 3.0 has become a repository of an ever growing variety of Web resources that include data and services associated with enterprises, social networks, sensors, cloud, as well as mobile and other devices that constitute the Internet of Things. These pose unprecedented challenges in terms of heterogeneity (variety), scale (volume), and continuous changes (velocity), as well as present corresponding opportunities if they can be exploited. Just as semantics has played a critical role in dealing with data heterogeneity in the past to provide interoperability and integration, it is playing an even more critical role in dealing with the challenges and helping users and applications exploit all forms of Web 3.0 data.

This book presents a unified approach to harness and exploit all forms of contemporary Web resources using the core principles of ability to associate meaning with data through conceptual or domain models and semantic descriptions including annotations, and through advanced semantic techniques for search, integration, and analysis. It discusses the use of Semantic Web standards and techniques when appropriate, but also advocates the use of lighter weight, easier to use, and more scalable options when they are more suitable. The authors' extensive experience spanning research and prototypes to development of operational applications and commercial technologies and products guide the treatment of the material.

KEYWORDS

semantic web, Web 3.0, machine-processable metadata, light-weight ontologies, semantic annotations, data integrations and interoperability, semantics in enterprises, semantic sensor web, semantic social web, social data analytics, semantic web services, semantics for cloud computing, dynamic ontology creation, semantics for Internet of Things, semantic enterprise applications, semantic web applications

To all my partners in gyan yoga at Kno.e.sis;
to my family members involved in gyan yoga—my daughters and their dadas.

– APS

To my family for their unwavering support.

– TKP

Contents

Preface

The value of semantics became clear to me when, in the late 1980s, I started to give tutorials on Heterogeneous Distributed Databases. I was trying to explain how the "cost of meal" in a restaurant can mean different things in different databases. The example was of my experience in eating a pizza at a restaurant in Venice in 1988. The pizza was advertised at 3,000 lira, but I ended up paying nearly 8,000 lira, given that the final cost included not only the menu cost of 3,000 lira but also two service charges and a tax. Depending on what add ons one includes, the meaning (semantics) of the "cost of meal" can vary. This early introduction to capturing meaning of data was followed by InfoHarness, a project we started in 1993 which is when the Web was still in its infancy, and Mozilla was the first browser. In its simplest form, we started associating types of metadata with heterogeneous forms of data and documents, and used a faceted (forms-based) interface for a browser-based search of documents on the Web and intranets. This was followed by a few research projects in the technology area, later termed semantic technology and Semantic Web. One interesting project was OBSERVER that started in 1995, which supported multi-ontology query processing, i.e., the resources could be annotated with different ontologies than the ontology used by a user to formulate a query (describe the query semantics with).

In 1999, I started Taalee (which was subsequently acquired by and merged into Voquette, Semagix, Fortent, and Actimize), which was perhaps the first Semantic Web/technology-based company. This book and the decade worth of subsequent research, applied and commercial work was based on simple principles that were captured in our publications, from a keynote in 2000, to a patent filed in 2000/awarded in 2001, and papers published since 2002. We (a) use pre-existing vocabularies and create ontologies, populated mostly automatically with limited human involvement by integrating multiple high quality data sources to fit the ontology schema, and use that to underpin semantics; (b) use vocabulary or ontology to semantically annotate (label) data in diverse syntax and structure (formats, media); and (c) build a variety of rich applications using semantic/faceted search, browsing, analysis, reasoning, and visualization. Step (a) is not very unlike what seems to be done for developing the Google Knowledge Base. In those days we used the term "Rich Media Objects" to describe meaningful data and metadata related to the object or entity that comes up in a result.

While the initial Web (Web 1.0) was still developing, its scope spread to intranets and enterprise data. Then came Web 2.0 that was dominated by user-generated content and social media. And as the Web evolved to what many call Web 3.0, more types of data, especially the sensor and mobile device generated data, became part of the Web ecosystem. At the LSDIS lab at the University of Georgia, and subsequently since 2007 at the Kno.e.sis Center at Wright State University, collaborations with students led to our applying the same basic principle to different types of data and their corresponding applications. These were described in a series of articles in IEEE Internet Computing, complemented by more technical research papers written by the students. Taalee/Voquette team members, esp. Krys Kochut, Brian Hammond, and Clemens Bertram were key collaborators in utilizing semantics for enterprise and Web documents. Kunal Verma and Karthik Gomadam were key collaborators in our work on semantic Web services. Meena Nagarajan and Karthik Gomadam were key collaborators in our efforts to use semantics and background knowledge for social (user-generated) data. Cory Henson has been a key collaborator for sensor data. Ajith Ranabahu collaborated on using semantics for achieving porting and interoperability across cloud platforms. Satya Sahoo was a collaborator on our provenance modeling work. Christopher Thomas was collaborator on our dynamic model creation (continuous semantics) work. It has been my pleasure and privilege to work with these young scholars.

Prof. Krishnaprasad Thirunarayan and I have collaborated on many of the above and other areas where semantics has enabled and empowered better search, integration, analysis, and reasoning involving a variety of resources that make up Web 3.0. Thus, he took over the mantle of synthesizing previous material that has involved extensive additions, revisions, and enhancement, making it possible for us to bring you this work.

Amit Sheth

My initial exposure to Semantic Web concepts was indirectly through its precursor—Semantic Networks—that was analyzed in my doctoral dissertation "The Semantics of Inheritance Networks." Specifically, the goal was to understand the semantics of instance-class-property networks in the presence of multiple inheritance and exceptions.

Subsequently, in the practical realm, we were faced with enriching human comprehensible technical documents and tables (actually, legacy materials and process specifications used in aerospace and automobile industries) to be machine comprehensible, to enable semi-automatic content extraction, integration, and manipulation. Surfacing the domain-specific content necessitated the development and use of controlled vocabularies and their hierarchical organization, annotation, and extraction tools, and underscored the significance of traceability for quality control. However, all this work predated Semantic Web as we know it today. In retrospect, Semantic Web standards, techniques, and tools, and the development of lightweight ontologies address exactly these practical challenges. Fortunately, this past experience has given me better appreciation of the benefits and the challenges that lie ahead for the realization of Web 3.0 at scale as we get swamped by data deluge.

I am grateful to Prof. Amit Sheth for inviting me to join him in developing this well-rounded resource by consolidating earlier research carried out with students at LSDIS and Kno.e.sis.

Krishnaprasad Thirunarayan

November 2012

CHAPTER 1

Role of Semantics and Metadata

We are facing a deluge of heterogeneous data created due to the widespread availability and use of personal computers, social media, mobile devices, and sensors, facilitated by accelerating progress in Web technologies, networking infrastructure, wireless communication, and cloud computing. Equally important is the democratization of content creation—instead of data created by few large organizations and the select few with computing resources for business, scientific, or engineering applications, with the advent of Web 2.0, anyone can create and share data. During the last two decades, the Internet and the Web became vehicles of sharing and using a large variety of Web resources. Figure 1.1 shows some of the key types of Web resources that have come into the limelight. Each of these Web resources have brought more types of heterogeneity and larger scalability chal-

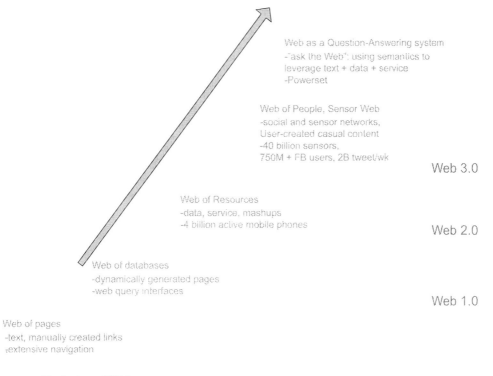

Figure 1.1: Evolution of Web.

lenges. Table 1.1[1] portrays the phenomenal growth of mobile devices [Nokia, 2008], social media, and sensors, all largely in the last five years. As a reference, note that there are about 1.6 billion

Table 1.1: Some of the ways data is generated
Data size estimates
5 billion mobile phone subscriptions [2010]
100 times use of mobile phone/day
4.1 billion actual actively used mobile phones [2010]
3.6 billion unique users with accounts and phones
4 billion users have SMS (up 19% in users)
1.9 billion users have MMS (up 21% in users)
1.4 billion use email on PC
3 billion users have camera phones
750+million Facebook users [1Q2011]
2 billion tweets/week [1Q2011]
500+K mobile applications
40+billion mobile sensors
250TB of sensor data for a NY-LA flight on B737

TV sets, 1.2 billion PCs and 4 billion tooth brushes in the world. Increasingly, data are created autonomously, such as through smart devices carried by humans and sensors connected to the Web. Figure 1.2[2] shows data growth trends. Figure 1.3[3] shows the evolution of the Web with the associated Web technologies. Specifically, it depicts the fact that, as time progresses, the connections between information is becoming explicit and more fine-grained, promoting personalization and more expressive social connections, eventually leading to robust collective intelligence.

No wonder the information overload or data deluge problem is going from bad to worse. We can no longer store all the data that are generated even if we wanted to. Nevertheless, these data are very valuable. We want to search them, browse them, integrate them, mine them, and ultimately use them to gain insight, develop situational awareness, discover new knowledge, answer difficult questions, and make decisions.

On the other hand, we have not taken comparable strides in tapping nuggets of information present in these data. The fundamental hurdle in this quest is our inability to automatically relate, disambiguate, understand, and abstract data, and distill them into knowledge that we can reliably reason with. *Semantics-empowered computing vision is about the use of machine processable semantics as a substrate to perform quality, reliable, distributed, and scalable analysis and reasoning with data.* This ability is essential for integration and visualization of data, and interoperability of services.

---

[1]http://research.nokia.com/people/john_shen, Facebook, Twitter.

[2]Higginbotham, S. (2010, September). Sensor Networks Top Social Networks for Big Data. Gigaom.com. http://gigaom.com/cloud/sensor-networks-top-social-networks-for-big-data-2/.

[3]Nova Spivack, 2007. http://www.radarnetworks.com.

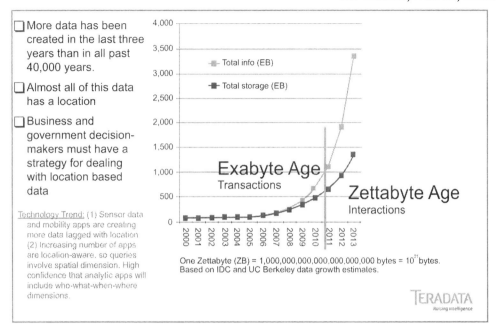

Figure 1.2: Data Growth Trends (see Footnote 2).

1.1   WEB 1.0, WEB 2.0, WEB 3.0

In the UNIX Workstation and PC Era predating the Web (1980's), the client-server paradigm was at the foundation of data sharing and social communication on the Internet. For each function, there was a separate server and client program. For example, FTP was used to share files, TELNET was used to access different machines, EMAIL was used for private communication, and USENET was used for public exchanges. The Standard Generalized Markup Language (SGML) was developed for defining markup languages for documents, where a markup describes a document's (domain-specific) structure and attributes. Invention of the World Wide Web (WWW) just over 20 years ago involved the concept of Uniform Resource Locator (URL) (that encodes name or location of a Web resource or service reflecting information such as communication protocol [http, telnet, ftp, mail, etc.], machine [IP address], and full-path address [in a directory]), that enabled an "integrated client" Web browser to manage interactions with different servers. HyperText Transmission Protocol (HTTP) was developed for text-based request-response communication between a client and a server. HyperText Markup Language (HTML), an application/instance of SGML, was developed for defining logical structure and presentation of documents.

Web 1.0, the Web of documents, refers to the first stage of the Web in which web pages were linked using hyperlinks, with Web browsers providing a convenient means to navigate through them. Web 1.0 came into being around 1989. By 1997, it grew to 1 million sites, and by 2004, to 50

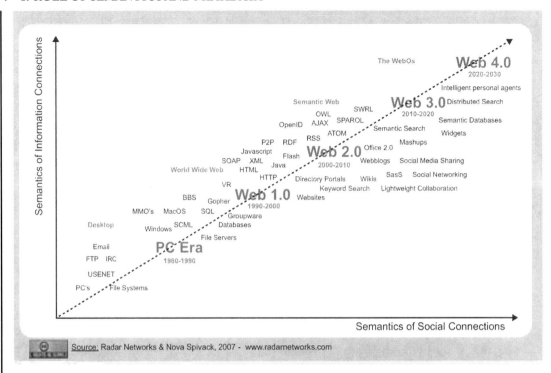

Figure 1.3: Evolution of Web Technologies.

million sites. The HTML documents (or pages) were either created manually and linked or were dynamically generated from databases. The existence of a link between two documents suggests a weak association between the linked documents, and the count of the incoming links can be used as a measure of attention the document gets or deserves. However, it is not always clear if the directional link is supportive or dismissive. In response to keyword-based queries, a search engine gleans relevance of a document using its content and authoritativeness of a document using the topology of the web of documents. The main form of semantics for the Web, largely consisting of pages in HTML, was the use of a human-created directory structure constructed by a small group of ontologists (in the case of Yahoo!) and an open source community (in the case of Open Directory Project) and manual cataloging of web pages and sites within that directory structure. Two of the earliest forms of associating semantics with Web-based data are through (a) defining metadata for data and websites, first developed by Meta Content Framework (MCF)[4] which was superseded by Resource Description Framework (RDF),[5] now the main language for representing semantic data, and (b) defining meaningful association between entities that may span documents or databases. As

---

[4]http://downlode.org/Etext/MCF/index.html
[5]http://www.w3.org/RDF/

a specific example, a form of semantic link called Metadata Reference Link (MREF) was described by associating metadata with hypertext link (using HREF) [Sheth et al., 2004].

Web 2.0 refers to the second stage in the evolution of the Web that enabled users to interact and collaborate with each other in a social media dialogue as consumers of user-generated content [OReilly, 2007]. Web 2.0 is generally assumed to have taken off around 2003. By 2006, there were 100 million websites, 9 billion web pages, and 1 billion global users. Web 2.0 consists of web of people and services. Examples of Web 2.0 include social networking sites, blogs, wikis, video sharing sites, hosted services, Web applications, mashups, folksonomies, etc. If Web 1.0 is "read web," which involved significant effort in creating a Web content, then Web 2.0 is "read/write web," which enabled any (even a casual) user to create content and easily share it. Examples of Web 2.0 technologies include XML (Extensible Markup Language that can be used to annotate documents or serialize data), AJAX (Asynchronous JavaScript and XML that enables Web applications to retrieve data from the server asynchronously without interfering with the existing page), JSON (JavaScript Object Notation, a lightweight data interchange format), RSS (Really Simple Syndication that allows subscription to feeds such as News, Events, Sports, etc.), and P2P (Peer to Peer) content sharing systems. As far as the semantics of the Web resources and their relationships are concerned, Web 2.0 supported the use of tags to describe various features. However, besides providing a rich interactive experience over the Web, and some ability for tag-based search of resources, Web 2.0 did not provide any significant additional power to meaningfully describe (or associate meaning with) data, and to reason with Web data and links. Applications employed pattern-based information retrieval techniques to summarize user-generated content, while mashups exploited spatio-temporal context to organize user-generated content. The social media succeeded in connecting and engaging people.

Web 3.0 refers to the third stage in the evolution of the Web that now has significant extension in the types of data, people, and interactions, along with heterogeneity and scale. Web 3.0 established itself starting 2006, and currently there are approximately 250 million websites and 32 billion web pages. Perhaps the most significant extension of the Web is the ability to connect a significant portion of humanity for the first time with over 5 billion mobile phones, of which over a billion and a half of the new connections have access to the Internet. This is complemented by more than 40 billion sensors covering increasingly large parts of the earth, constantly reporting on human activities and environmental information. Figure 1.1 depicts the evolution of the Web—from Web 1.0 to Web 3.0.

In summary: Web 1.0 is about democratization of web page creation, publishing and consumption. Web 2.0 is about democratization of journalism and commentary, community engagement, and Web services. Web 3.0 is about democratized analysis, semantic search, and answer-extraction from high granularity linked data web [Idehen, 2012].

Much of the power of new information processing capability comes from the ability to integrate and analyze this heterogeneous and large amount of data. Standards-based techniques and tools for machine-processable semantics are the enablers for this. Semantics processing that now finds widespread use in Web 3.0 started to take shape in the 1990's, with the introduction of ontologies to represent semantics of a domain in 1993 [Gruber, 1995], development of RDF, and coining of the term *Semantic Web* to discuss the use of metadata to describe data on the Web [Berners-Lee and Fischetti, 2001]. Specifically, Berners-Lee and Fischetti [2001] noted that "if HTML and the Web made all the online documents look like one huge book, RDF, schema, and inference languages will make all the data in the world look like one huge database." Berners-Lee also said "I have a dream for the Web [in which computers] become capable of analyzing all the data on the Web—the content, links, and transactions between people and computers." A "Semantic Web," which should make this possible, has yet to emerge, but when it does, the day-to-day mechanisms of trade, bureaucracy, and our daily lives will be handled by machines talking to machines. The "intelligent agents" people have touted for ages will finally materialize.

The semantics is captured by specifying unary relations (classes) instances on Web resources and entities, and binary relations (properties) instances between Web resources, entities, and primitive values. This is accomplished by providing coherent machine-processable designators (called Universal Resource Locators or URLs) for the Web resources, entities, and their relations, formal encoding of relation instances (ABox), and optionally axioms characterizing these relations or conceptual schemas (TBox) [Antoniou and van Harmelen, 2004, Reynolds, 2001]. The relation instances describe and link Web resources and entities, provide context, and enable reasoning with them mechanically. *In essence, the Semantic Web promotes assimilation of meaning to extract or construct an answer as opposed to retrieving a document that has the potential to contain the answer.* Thus, machine-accessible semantics is expected to enable reliable analysis, disambiguation, integration, query answering, abstraction, and maintenance of heterogeneous data. Furthermore, Semantic Web standards developed by the World Wide Web Consortium (W3C) are now supported by robust technologies and are in wide use. See [Domingue et al., 2011] for further discussions on Semantic Web foundations and technologies.

Rapid penetration of social and sensor networks has accelerated the participation of people and machines to complement and collaborate with each other, by promoting intelligent agents and applications that exploit both social connections and embedded sensors in a cyber-physical world. Social and sensor data analytics involves spatio-temporal-thematic reasoning for interpreting and mapping machine-generated quantitative information into human accessible qualitative/textual form, and for assisting identification of entities and their relationships to understand situations and events. The future will yield technologies for distributed semantic search and semantics-empowered social and sensor data integration, and facilitate construction of intelligent personal agents and cyber-physical systems. Let's now review the reasons semantics will play a central role in Web 3.0 and beyond.

Semantics for integration: Semantics, in the sense of archiving shared understanding and meaning, comes from agreement. Consequently, we have long seen its role in integrating data in heterogeneous syntax and structure. More recently, it is playing an increasing role in integrating information about the same concept or object in a different modality and media—for example, to relate a person's image with his or her descriptive information, or to correlate information about an event on social media with corresponding sensor observations. In coming years, semantics will play a crucial role in integrating objects that straddle the cyber-physical or physical-virtual divide.

Semantics for intelligent processing: Much attention in the past has focused on data and information search and browsing in which the complexity of processing is reduced because of significant human involvement in interpreting the results. As we move up the information processing value chain from search and browsing, to integration and analysis, to situational awareness and question-answering, the complexity of information processing increases significantly. Looking at it from another perspective, information processing has started to move from keyword-based processing to object-based processing, and on to relationship- and event-centric processing. Relationships are at the heart of semantics, and fundamentally, the computations will need to focus on modeling, processing, and exploiting relationships [Sheth et al., 2004]. When it is possible to use formal languages, this will involve better use of inductive, deductive, and abductive reasoning.

Semantics for knowledge-enabled computing: The power of human reasoning not only comes from the sophistication of the computing our brain supports, but also from the use of background knowledge and past experiences. Similarly, there is now a rapidly growing use of application of background knowledge in improving information processing—from improving information extraction, NLP, and Machine Learning, to better understanding and processing social and sensor data. We are now able to apply domain-independent (e.g., related to time, space, and geographic concepts) to domain-specific models of various complexities and comprehensiveness such as nomenclatures, taxonomies, and ontologies, to improve information processing. The ability to utilize user- and community-created dictionaries (e.g., Urban dictionary[6]) and knowledge repositories (e.g., MusicBrainz[7]), and to exploit structured information from unstructured data (e.g., DBpedia from Wikipedia[8]), and to reuse such knowledge in improving computation has added significant strength to semantic processing.

Semantics for abstractions and experience: The increasing amount of data generated by 5 billion mobile phone users (many now with data connections), millions of social media users, and 40+ billion mobile sensors, are finding their way onto the Web. A single 4-hour flight might generate 240 terabytes of data. How much of this data are useful for a given human need? The ability to search this amount of data, however good, is simply not scalable in terms of human consumption of search results. What we care for are a few nuggets of information or insights that we can act upon. We care about the broader and aggregate understanding of events, improved decision making, and getting answers to our questions. And we care about enhancing our human experience. Semantics is a core component of developing the abstraction mechanisms so that we can use computing to support perception and cognition. Semantic approaches that support abstractions convert low-level data and observations into high-level symbolic representation that constitute our perception and cognition. Semantics-empowered solutions are now able to analyze constantly streaming sensor and/or social

---

[6]http://www.urbandictionary.com/
[7]http://musicbrainz.org/
[8]http://dbpedia.org/About

data to tell us abstractions and events of human interests (e.g., icy roads, blizzard conditions, need for intervention to save crops, chances that a movie will succeed, progress of a mass protest); check Kno.e.sis demos for some examples (see `http://knoesis.org/showcase`).

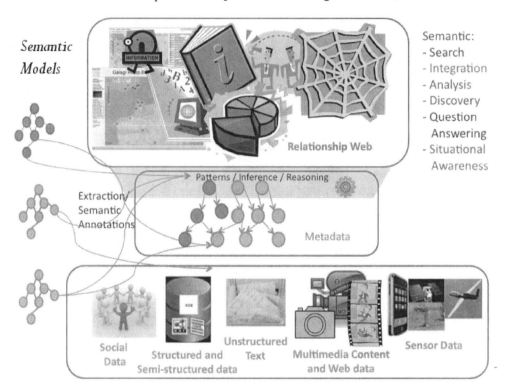

Figure 1.4: Semantics provides the glue for integration and analysis of heterogeneous data for comprehensive situational awareness, question answering, and knowledge discovery. Semantic models abstract and formalize domain-specific (e.g., medical, government, etc.) and domain-independent (e.g., spatial, temporal, etc.) concepts and relationships. The metadata extracted from the data and materialized as annotations makes the semantics of data explicit for pattern discovery and reasoning [Sheth, 2010] (copyright © IEEE, with permission).

Figure 1.4 shows the central approach to utilizing semantics in Web 3.0. Semantics provides the glue for integration and analysis of heterogeneous data for comprehensive situational awareness, question answering and knowledge discovery. It has three main components: (a) semantic models including domain-independent (e.g., time and space) and domain-specific (e.g., medical, government, etc.) models, based on formal ontologies or informal crowd-sourced labels (see Chapter 2); (b) semantic metadata extraction and annotation of any form of data; and (c) semantic processing in various forms such as pattern and association discovery, inference, and reasoning to develop semantic solutions (that is, semantic versions of search, integration, analysis, discovery, situational awareness, and question answering), etc. Semantic models abstract and formalize essential concepts and relationships in a range of domains spanning application areas such as medicine, transportation, and motion sensing, to general cross-cutting areas such as spatial and temporal. The semantic metadata (annotations) extracted from the data makes explicit the semantics in a "standard" form to facilitate robust machine processing for data integration, pattern mining, complex querying, reasoning, and answer extraction.

This book is organized as follows: Chapter 2 discusses various types of semantics ranging from informal and consensus-based to formal and rigorous, and different ways of specifying them reflecting efficiency-expressive power tradeoff. It also provides some guidelines on ontology development. Chapter 3 discusses various forms of data and services, and different approaches to their semantic enrichment via annotation. In the subsequent chapters, we describe different forms of data, the role of semantics for data analytics, techniques for creating semantic metadata, and sample applications of relevant semantic technologies. Chapter 4 deals with the application of semantics to enterprise data and eScience. Chapter 5 deals with semantics of services. Chapter 6 and Chapter 7 deal with semantics for sensor data and social data respectively. Chapter 8 deals with semantics for cloud computing. Chapter 9 introduces advanced semantic applications that will fuel future research.

CHAPTER 2

Types and Models of Semantics

Enabling applications that exploit heterogeneous data in the Semantic Web will require us to harness a broad variety of semantics. Considering the role of semantics in a number of research areas in computer science, we organize semantics into three forms: *implicit, formal*, and *powerful* [Sheth et al., 2005b], and explore their role in enabling some of the key capabilities related to the Semantic Web. We view different semantic formalisms through the lens of an expressivity-efficiency continuum to better appreciate their relative merits and limitations.

Information Retrieval (IR) is finding material (usually documents) of an unstructured nature (usually text) that satisfies an information need from within large collections (usually stored on computers) [Manning et al., 2008]. Information Extraction (IE) deals with automatic extraction of structured information from unstructured and/or semi-structured machine-readable documents. Computational Linguistics (CL) is an interdisciplinary field dealing with the statistical or rule-based modeling of natural language from a computational perspective [Wikipedia, 2011]. Information retrieval, information extraction, and computational linguistics techniques primarily draw upon analysis of unstructured texts and document repositories that have a loosely defined structure. In these sorts of data sources, the semantics is *implicit*. Machines can analyze implicit semantics with several, mostly statistical, techniques. However, in the fields of Knowledge Representation (KR), several subareas of Artificial Intelligence (AI), and Databases (DB), the data representation takes a more formal, structured, and rigid form. Well-defined syntax with definite semantic interpretation is used to represent knowledge and conceptualization. There are also definite syntax-driven semantic rules to represent the meaning of complex syntactic structures. Such techniques constitute the *formal semantics*. Efforts related to formal semantics have spanned a wide gamut of logic-based formalisms, from relational algebra/calculus to first-order logic (FOL) to Horn logic to non-monotonic logics, and have traded expressiveness for acceptable computational characteristics. Most of the attention in the Semantic Web community has centered on variants of first-order logic—the Description Logic (DL) [Baader, 2003] and the Web Ontology Language (OWL) [Hitzler et al., 2009a,b]. Specifically, OWL is a family of knowledge representation languages for authoring ontologies that has been endorsed by the W3C. These approaches view the world in terms of crisp concepts and relationships among entities that are either true or false. In contrast, there are concepts and relationships that are intrinsically fuzzy or uncertain due to incompleteness in our knowledge about them, and they happen to hold to various degrees of membership or levels of certainty [Zadeh, 1996]. Such semantics are referred to as *powerful*, and it has been the province of soft computing [Sanchez, 2006]. Similar concerns about the diversity of semantics have also been echoed by various other researchers. For instance, Uschold [2003] has discussed a semantic continuum involving informal to formal and implicit to explicit, and Gruber [2003] has talked about informal, semi-formal, and formal ontologies. Woods [2004] has emphasized the limitations of the FOL (and hence DL) in the context of natural language understanding, and Zadeh [2005] has discussed the limitations of bivalent logic in the context of question answering.

Furthermore, in order to interpret data of any kind, we need a model of semantics and a means to associate semantics with the data. Ultimately, providing semantics to data involves understanding entities, actions, and relationships the data describe, and making explicit relationships that are implicit using reasoning. In fact, querying data involves verifying or seeking entities that satisfy certain relationships. Furthermore, when the data are distributed or shared among various data producers and data consumers, it is also necessary to have a shared semantics through common vocabulary to specify entities, concepts, and relationships, or through mappings between different local vocabularies. *Ontology* refers to shared vocabulary and semantics, while *ontology alignment* refers to mediating between different but related ontologies. Section 2.4 discusses various facets of ontology and ontology development in detail.

Ultimately, the purpose is to capture semantic equivalence among different vocabularies through purely syntactic means as much as possible for automation, with the Holy Grail being the pursuit of common vocabulary to reduce semantic equivalence to syntactic equality. (For example, a table of synonymous terms provides a collection of syntactically distinct but semantically equivalent terms. In arithmetic, syntactically distinct numerals and expressions such as 25, 5*5, $125 - 100$, $(30 + 1)$ in octal and $(1A - 1)$ in hex, can be shown to be semantically equivalent, that is, signifying the same number 25 (in decimal), by specifying axioms for the operations and deriving rewrite/transformation rules for expression evaluation.) In practice, there are several approaches to model semantics based on the amount of detail we can or wish to capture.

Depending on the chosen model of semantics, we can either use annotations (that is, comments or metadata) to embed semantics within the data (e.g., using microformats), or provide a separate translation of the data into a target semantic formalism (e.g., FOL, OWL). In the former approach, the data and its interpretation are closely intertwined, while in the latter approach, there is an additional need to provide a separate correspondence between the original data and its translation, for traceability. There is also a third approach that tries to marry the benefits of both these approaches by automatically generating a translation of the embedded annotations into a target semantic formalism. For example, RDFa (or Resource Description Framework in attributes) is a W3C Recommendation that adds a set of attribute-level extensions to XHTML for embedding rich metadata within Web documents [Hausenblas et al., 2008], while GRDDL (or Gleaning Resource Descriptions from Dialects of Languages) is a technique for obtaining RDF data from XHTML pages [Connoly, 2007, Halpin and Davis, 2007].

2.1   TYPES OF SEMANTICS

In this section, we give a brief, informal overview of the three types of semantics identified above.

2.1.1   IMPLICIT SEMANTICS

This type of semantics is implicit in the patterns in data and is not represented explicitly in any strict machine processable syntax or available for human scrutiny. Examples of this sort of semantics are found in the following scenarios:

- Co-occurrence of documents or terms in the same cluster after a clustering process is complete. Note that the implicit patterns depend on the chosen representation of documents, similarity/distance metric, and cluster fusion criterion [Manning et al., 2008].

- A document linked to another document via a hyperlink, potentially associating semantic metadata describing the concepts that relate the two documents. For example, semantic metadata in the form of a hyperlink can annotate a word in a document to link it to its definition on Wikipedia.

- The sort of semantics implied by two documents belonging to categories that are siblings of each other in a concept hierarchy.

- Automatic classification of a document to broadly indicate what a document is about with respect to a chosen taxonomy; keyword-based summarization of a document; searching and disambiguating entities (does the word "palm" in a document refer to a palm tree, the palm of your hand, or a palm-top computer?)

- Bioinformatics applications that exploit patterns like sequence alignment, or secondary and tertiary protein structure analysis.

One may argue that although there is no strict syntactic and explicit representation of the semantics, the knowledge about patterns in data may yet be machine processable. For instance, it is possible to get a numeric similarity judgment between documents in a corpus. However, it is not possible to look at documents and automatically infer the presence of a named relationship between concepts in the documents. Basically, machine learning techniques such as clustering, concept-learning, and rule-learning, Hidden Markov Models, Artificial Neural Networks, and others exploit implicit semantics. These techniques can also be found in early steps toward the Semantic Web, such as clustering in Yippy (formerly Vivisimo's Clusty search engine), as well as in early Semantic Web products, such as metadata extraction on Web Fountain technology [Dill et al., 2003], automatic classification, and metadata extraction in Semagix Freedom [Sheth et al., 2002].

2.1.2   FORMAL SEMANTICS

Computers lack the ability to understand and disambiguate natural language, so it is infeasible to use natural language as a means for machines to communicate with each other. Formal semantics refers to describing the semantics of a language in purely symbolic terms that is accessible to machines. The semantics is defined inductively on the syntax of a language, and the logical consequence relation is formalized in a proof system in terms of axioms and proof rules. There are some necessary and sufficient features that make a language and its semantics formal. These features include:

- *The Notion of Model Theoretic Semantics*: Primitive symbols (atoms, n-ary function symbols, and n-ary predicate symbols) in a formal language are interpreted using semantic structures (domain of discourse D, n-ary functions over D, and n-ary relations over D) that reflect certain basic presuppositions about the "nature of the world" that are implicitly described by the language. Expressions in the form of terms are mapped to the domain of discourse, and sentences are used as constraints to define models. The logical consequence of a set of sentences S is the set of sentences T that are true in all models of S.

- *The Principle of Compositionality*: The meaning of an expression is defined in terms of the meanings of its immediate parts and of the way they are syntactically combined. The emphasis is on locality and referential transparency.

From a less technical perspective, formal semantics means machine-processable semantics, which is precise and unambiguous. Examples of such semantics are:

- The semantics of subsumption in DLs, reflecting the human tendency of categorizing by means of broader or narrower descriptions.

- The semantics of partonomy, accounting for what is part of an object, not which category the object belongs to.

- The semantics of FOL used to formalize classical mathematics.

2.1.3   POWERFUL (SOFT) SEMANTICS

Statistical techniques give us great insight into a corpus of documents or a large collection of data in general, when a program exists that can actually pose the right questions to the data. All derived relationships are statistical in nature and we only have the likelihood of their validity. In contrast, traditional knowledge representation formalisms derive certain knowledge from explicitly stated certain knowledge. Logical deduction is truth preserving. Furthermore, the restriction of expressiveness to a subset of FOL (such as in DLs) allows the system to verify the consistency of its knowledge.

However, as the size of the knowledge base increases, and as knowledge from many sources is added, it is difficult to guarantee consistency. In such situations, it becomes desirable to develop systems that are robust with respect to inconsistencies. *That is, the system must be able to identify sources of inconsistency and localize its effects, rather than allow inconsistency to corrupt reasoning from the entire knowledge-base.* In order to deal with this, we need to adapt bi-valued logics and KR languages, taking inspiration from how humans reason in the fahausenblasision, uncertainty, inconsistencies, partial truth, and approximation. Major approaches to reasoning with imprecision are: 1) probabilistic reasoning, 2) possibilistic reasoning [Dubois et al., 1994], and 3) fuzzy reasoning [Zadeh, 1996].

Other formalisms have focused on resolving local inconsistencies in knowledge bases using annotated/paraconsistent logics (see [Blair and Subrahmanian, 1989, Cao, 2000, Kifer and Subrahmanian, 1992, Lukasiewicz, 2005, Thirunarayan and Kifer, 1993]) and to provide more natural representation formalisms using extensions to fuzzy logics (see [Straccia, 1998, 2004]). Koller et al. [1997] and others have developed probabilistic description logics [Heinsohn, 1994, Jaeger, 1994] and Bayesian-style inference on OWL [Pan et al., 2005]. The combination of probabilistic and fuzzy knowledge under one representation mechanism is proposed by [Zadeh, 2002]. In fact, different formalisms can co-exist harmoniously with each other, given that they are designed to address different issues—incompleteness in knowledge, randomness in the phenomenon, intrinsically multi-valued concepts, or non-crisp concepts with fuzzy membership. These formalisms can be "complementary rather than competitive." Furthermore, deduction (such as predicting effects from causes) is not the only form of reasoning that is of interest. Instead, we also need to consider abduction (such as explaining effects using possible causes) and induction (such as learning causal rules from correlated observations). Bayesian type reasoning is a way to do abduction by virtue of applying probabilities.

A major drawback of logics dealing with uncertainties is the required assignment of prior probabilities and/or fuzzy membership functions. Obviously, there are two ways of doing that—manual assignment by domain experts and automatic assignment using machine learning techniques. Manual assignments can be arbitrary and tedious, even if the expert has profound knowledge of the domain. Automatic assignments of prior values require a large and representative dataset of annotated instances, and finding or agreeing on what is a representative set is difficult or at times impossible. Often, however, the probability values for relationships can be obtained from the dataset using statistical methods, thus we categorize these relationships as implicit semantics.

So far, powerful semantics and soft computing research has found little use in the context of developing the Semantic Web. In our opinion, for this vision to become a reality, it will be necessary to go beyond RDFS (a schema language for declaring classes and types for describing the terms used in RDF) and OWL, and work toward standardized formalisms that support powerful semantics. In the end, powerful semantics will combine the benefits of hierarchical composition of knowledge and statistical analysis; deductive, abductive, and inductive reasoning; and match an approach with the nature of knowledge, rather than limiting the set of admissible approaches. For example, we discuss how to encode restricted cause-effect (disease-symptom) relationships pertinent to medical diagnosis in OWL and identify a special case of abduction that can be carried by an OWL reasoner [Henson et al., 2011]. We further generalized this by formalizing the perception cycle, which essentially combines deductive and abductive reasoning in an integrated framework for deriving actionable explanation by systematically refining hypotheses by seeking additional observations in a targeted, tractable fashion.

2.2 APPLICATIONS AND TYPES OF SEMANTICS THEY EXPLOIT

Ontologies have found applications in a number of areas including knowledge engineering and management, natural language processing, e-commerce, and intelligent information integration [Fensel, 2000]. Due to their independence from lower-level data models, ontologies are a natural candidate for integrating heterogeneous databases [Kashyap and Sheth, 1994], enabling interoperability among disparate systems, and specifying interfaces to independent, knowledge-based services. We discuss a sampling of application areas and types of semantics they use. Note that expressivity of a representation language (to be discussed in the next section) does not necessarily correspond to the naturalness and the richness of real world that can be captured by the conceptual model. With higher expressivity of representational language, the domain being modelled can be captured in finer details and allows computational system (that is, reasoning system) to support more in-depth processing capability, but requires sometimes shredding nuances of the real world being modelled.

2.2.1 RETRIEVAL APPLICATIONS: INFORMATION VS. DATA

Data retrieval (DR) aims at determining all objects that satisfy a semantically well-defined query, while information retrieval (IR) aims to decipher user information need and interpret document content in order to satisfy a query. Matching between a document and a query in the abstracted space of the set of index words (which exemplifies IR) is very imprecise, while relational database and its query language (which exemplifies DR) has semantic clarity and precision. Ideally, document querying can be transitioned to DR if only we could re-author all the documents so as to provide formal semantics to them and implement a sufficiently powerful query language. Semantic Web is a via media, intermediate step that provides a practical approach to approximating document semantics for coarse-grained retrieval using ontologies and annotations.

Table 2.1: Information Retrieval vs. Data Retrieval [Thirunarayan and Immaneni, 2009]

Aspect	Information Retrieval	Data Retrieval
Data:	Unstructured; open to interpretation	Structured with well-defined semantics
Query:	Usually incomplete or ambiguous w.r.t. information need	Well-defined semantics
Results Quality:	Partial match allowed; relevance-based ranking	Exact match required - no or many results possible
Foundations:	Probabilistic underpinnings	Algebra/Logic
Application:	Search engines; Library	Accounting

Table 2.1 summarizes the fundamental differences between IR and DR. IR usually applies to unstructured data that are open to interpretation, while DR applies to structured data with well-

defined meaning. IR queries are usually incomplete or ambiguous with respect to information need, and the results are ordered using relevance-based ranking to enable partial matches. DR queries, on the other hand, have well-defined meaning requiring an exact match; however, they are fragile in that they can lead to no results or too many results with respect to information need. IR has a probabilistic foundation, while DR has algebraic/logic underpinnings. A typical application of IR is a search engine, while that of DR is an accounting system.

First generation search engines such as Aliweb retrieved documents that matched keyword-based queries. Second generation search engines such as Excite, Lycos, and Altavista incorporated content-specific relevance ranking based on a vector space model (TF-IDF) to hone in on a relevant subset of documents in spite of high recall [Manning et al., 2008]. To overcome spamming, and to exploit collective Web wisdom, third generation search engines such as Google, Yahoo!, and Bing incorporated content-independent, source authority information using a PageRank algorithm [Brin and Page, 1998] and notions of hubs and authorities [Kleinberg, 1999], and attempted to glean relative semantic emphasis of various words based on syntactic features, such as fonts, and distance between query term hits. Contemporary search engines have also incorporated context, annotations, user profiles, and past query history associated with a user to personalize the search and apply additional reasoning to improve satisfaction of the information need [Guha et al., 2003]. distinguish navigational searches, where a user provides a phrase to be found in a document, and re-search searches, where a user provides a phrase to designate an object. Jansen et al. [2008] later refined these searches as navigational, informational, and transactional. Early semantic search engines such as Taalee/MediaAnywhere, Voquette/SCORE, and Semagix/Freedom [Sheth et al., 2001, 2002] used ontologies and background knowledge for semantic metadata extraction and faceted semantic search that exploit entities and relationships. More recently, major search engines have started to exploit large background knowledge bases, parts of which are based on a structured knowledge extracted from a community-created corpus (e.g., Wikipedia) and domain-specific structured datasets represented as linked data using Semantic Web technologies. Although details are not publicly discussed, the Yahoo! initiative of developing ConceptBase, Bing's incorporation of Powerset technology which extracts entities and relationships from Wikipedia, and Google's acquisition of Freebase point to the type of background knowledge being exploited. Some, like Bing, are more aggressively creating a domain-specific entity or knowledge base and support limited forms of faceted search. Emerging semantic search engines, and their "intelligent" counterparts—question-answering systems—benefit from all three forms of semantics [Ferrucci et al., 2010].

2.2.2   DATA MINING APPLICATIONS

The statistical analysis of data allows the exploration of relationships that are not explicitly stated. Data mining finds non-trivial patterns in unstructured and structured data. As discussed earlier, flat/hierarchical clustering (unsupervised learning) and classification (supervised learning), group and optionally tag similar entities or objects based on some notion of similarity of the representations [Manning et al., 2008]. The hierarchy with summary tags can be used to obtain a taxonomy semi-automatically [Kashyap et al., 2005]. Association rule mining enables gleaning of formal association rules implicit in the attribute-value patterns in a relational database [Agrawal and Srikant, 1994, Agrawal et al., 1993].

2.2.3   ANALYTICAL APPLICATIONS

Future search engines will be expected to extract an answer to a query rather than serve a collection of documents that is likely to contain an answer. They will also be required to query vast repositories of metadata to improve precision, recall, and reliability of the answer. As described by [Anyanwu and Sheth, 2002], "semantic associations" capture complex relationships between entities involving sequences of predicates (Boolean functions) and sets of predicate sequences that interact in complex ways. Since the predicates are semantic metadata extracted from heterogeneous multi-source documents, this is an attempt to discover complex relationships between objects described or mentioned in those documents. Detecting such associations is at the heart of many research and analytical activities that are crucial to applications in national security and business intelligence. The datasets that semantic associations operate over are RDF/RDFS graphs. The semantics of a link connecting two nodes in an RDF/RDFS graph are implicit, in the sense that there is no explicit interpretation of the semantics of the link other than the fact that it is a predicate in a statement (except for rdfs:subPropertyOf or links that represent data type properties—for which there is Model-Theoretic [Formal] semantics). Hence, the RDF/RDFS graph is composed of a combination of implicit and formal semantics. The objective of semantic associations is therefore to find all contextually relevant link sequences that relate two entities. This is, in effect, an attempt to combine the implicit and formal semantics of the links in the RDF/RDFS graph in conjunction with the context of the query, to determine the multifaceted (multivalent) semantics of a set of "connections" between entities. We view these multivalent semantics as a form of powerful semantics. In the context of search, semantic associations can be thought of as a class of research searches or discovery style searches.

2.3   MODELS OF SEMANTICS

Informally, a semantic model is a way to abstract and relate different pieces of information. Normally, it consists of objects and concepts, and relationships among them. Semantic models (and the associated representational languages) can be broadly divided into two categories: prescriptive and descriptive, which can be further refined on the basis of their expressive power.

2.3.1   PRESCRIPTIVE APPROACHES SUMMARY

Prescriptive approaches enable specification of formal semantics of symbols from scratch. Relational algebra/calculus [Ramakrishnan and Gehrke, 2002], description logics [Baader, 2003], OWL [Hitzler et al., 2009b], first-order logic, well-founded semantics of logic programs, modal logics, etc., are all well-known examples of this approach. Specifically, in each case, the meaning of symbols representing concepts and relationships is captured unambiguously through the sentences in the language of logic, and sound inferences can be mechanically derived. On the other hand, the "completeness" of inferences depends on how accurately a specification mirrors or can mirror the real-world concepts and relationships. In any case, these approaches clearly specify, in purely symbolic terms, expected answers to queries and inferences. For example, at one extreme, axiomatic specification of data types formalize axioms that operators/functions of a type must satisfy [Guttag et al., 1993]. These provide a means to mechanize semantic equivalence in terms of syntactic equality, that is, two expressions/terms are semantically equivalent (mean the same) if and only if they can be proven so using the axioms provided. (This sort of reasoning is known as equational reasoning.) In general, the level of axiomatization of predicates determines how accurate the axiomatization is in faithfully representing a specific interpretation (e.g., model of arithmetic, real-world concepts/relationships). These axiomatizations have long served as a foundation for variants of first-order logic theorem provers (e.g., automatic provers such as Boyer-Moore's NQTHM, or semi-automatic interactive proof assistants such as LARCH, PVS, Higher Order Logic (HOL), or OWL reasoners). In fact, the sequence of formalisms, starting from relational algebra, to Horn logic, to description logics, to first-order logic, to modal logics, clearly illustrate tradeoffs between expressive power and computational efficiency/feasibility.

First-Order Logic and Modal Logics
First-order logic deals with objects, functions, and relationships. It provides syntax for specifying functions and relationships through terms and well-formed formulae involving Boolean operators (and, or, not, implies, etc.) and quantifiers (universal and existential). It defines notions of semantic structure, interpretation, satisfaction, model, and Herbrand model to provide semantics to the language and make precise the notion of logical consequence or deduction. Godel's Completeness theorem shows that theoremhood is computable/semidecidable (by providing a proof system [axioms and inference rules] to recursively enumerate theorems), and Godel's Incompleteness theorem shows that enumerating truths in the model of arithmetic is not recursively enumerable (undecidable). Modal logics introduce two modalities into first-order logic, called possibility and necessity, for capturing different "strengths of truths." Subtly different interpretations of modalities are formalized through different axioms. Kripke generalized the FOL model theory for modal logics by interpreting modalities in terms of reachability relation among possible worlds (first-order structures).

Relational Algebra/Calculus
Relational algebra deals with finitary relations and five primitive closure operators: the selection, the projection, the Cartesian product, the set union, and the set difference. Codd [1970] proposed such an algebra as a basis for database query languages, and showed that it is essentially equivalent in expressive power to relational calculus (a limited fragment of first-order logic). Furthermore, relation queries can be computed efficiently.

Horn Logic and Logic Programming

Horn logic serves as the foundation of logic programming languages. Horn clauses are a restricted form of FOL conjunctive normal form syntax where each clause has at most one positive literal. Datalog, which is Horn clauses without function symbols, is more expressive than relational algebra because Datalog can define transitive closure of a binary relation while relational algebra cannot. Compared to FOL, Horn logic can be effectively mechanized. In fact, top-down interpreters with tabling and bottom-up interpreters with magic sets optimization are restricted forms of refutation-based FOL theorem provers that are very efficient for processing Boolean queries and answer extraction queries. In the context of Artificial Intelligence (AI), Horn logic can be thought of as generalization of AND-OR trees and state-space search in AI, and in the context of compilers, they can mechanize attribute grammars (via definite clause grammars). With stratified negation-as-failure operator, logic programming languages also provide a computational platform for knowledge representation and (non-monotonic) reasoning.

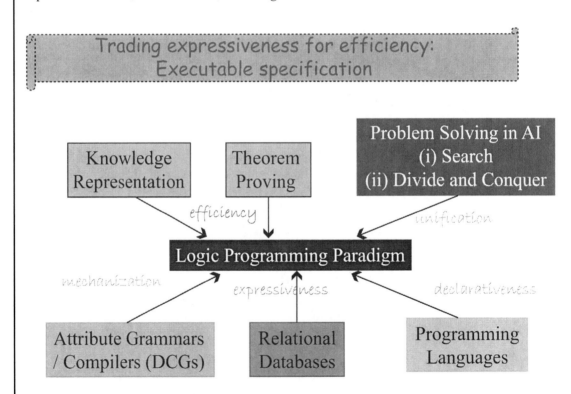

Figure 2.1: Applications of Logic Programming

Resource Description Framework (RDF) and Schema (RDFS)

RDF is a standard data model for defining unary and binary relation instances. For example, the facts that "John is a person" and "Susan is John's mother" can be described in RDF and encoded using XML in <http://www.example.org/> namespace as:

```
<rdf:RDF xmlns:rdf="http://www.w3.org/1999/02/22-rdf-syntax-ns#"
xmlns:ns="http://www.example.org/#">
  <ns:Person rdf:about="http://www.example.org/#john">
    <ns:hasMother rdf:resource="http://www.example.org/#susan" />
  </ns:Person>
</rdf:RDF>
```

Originally, the emphasis was on using RDF for describing metadata for Web resources, but later its wider applicability has been realized. Specifically, RDF statements can be used to define class (unary relation) instances, property (binary relation) instances, collections, and properties about RDF statements through reification. These are also called ABox or assertional knowledge.

RDFS specifies information about standard properties (type, domain, range, subclass, sub-property, etc.) used in the vocabulary of RDF. These properties are used to define other vocabulary terms such as by specifying class and property inheritance hierarchies. These are also called TBox or terminological knowledge. For example, the RDFS assertion that "PassengerVehicle is a MotorVehicle" can be encoded in XML as

```
<rdf:Description ID="PassengerVehicle">
    <rdf:type resource="http://www.w3.org/2000/01/rdf-schema#Class"/>
    <rdfs:subClassOf rdf:resource="#MotorVehicle"/>
</rdf:Description>
```

Description Logics (DLs) and Web Ontology Language (OWL)

Description logics (DLs) are a family of restricted FOL languages that are more expressive than propositional logic but are more tractable than first-order logic. Specifically, theoremhood in DLs is decidable [Tobies, 2001]. OWL is a family of knowledge representation languages for modeling ontologies that is a culmination of two earlier concurrent efforts called the DARPA Agent Markup Language (DAML) Program and Ontology Inference/Interchange Layer (OIL). OWL comes in three flavors, called species, to provide different expressivity/computational efficiency trade-offs: OWL-Full, OWL-DLs, and OWL-Lite. OWL-DLs can be further refined on the basis of the constraints and the closure characteristics of the concepts (classes) and the roles (properties) they support. OWL-DLs (Web Ontology Language-DL) can be viewed as machine-processable standardization of DLs for interoperability and scalability that promotes reuse of data and reasoning infrastructure over the Web. OWL-DLs overlap with RDF/RDFS in that both can use RDF formatted data and share common classes and predicates. However, OWL-DLs also simplify and regularize RDF formal semantics by abolishing reification, and enrich RDFS by providing more expressive primitives (e.g., subsumption, inverse, transitivity, and cardinality constraints) to facilitate axiomatization. OWL2 further includes constructs for expressiveness and syntactic sugars for convenience by defining three different profiles: OWL 2 EL, OWL 2 QL, and OWL 2 RL with useful computational properties for scalability and interoperability.

An Aside

Recently, DLs have become the dominant formalism for knowledge representation. Although DLs have gained substantial popularity, some of their fundamental properties can be seen as drawbacks when viewed in the context of its future. The formal semantics of DLs are based on set theory. A concept in DLs is interpreted as a set of things that share one required common feature. Relationships between concepts or roles are interpreted as a subset of the cross-product of the domain of interpretation. This leaves no scope for the representation of degrees of concept membership or uncertainty associated with concept membership. Although DLs present a favorable trade-off between computational complexity and expressive power, there are still fundamental issues with respect to the inability of DLs to allow for representation of non-monotonicity, fuzzy and probabilistic knowledge.

Besides general purpose reasoners discussed above, there are a host of special purpose reasoners for dealing with inheritance hierarchies (equivalently, hyponymy/hypernymy, or ISA relationship), partonomy hierarchies (equivalently, meronymy/holonymy or, HAS-A relationship), etc. For instance, inheritance reasoning is well-understood and tractable when confined to tree-structured class hierarchies with individuals and properties (including exceptions) and for Directed Acyclic Graph (DAG)-structured multiple inheritance hierarchies, which appear naturally in object-oriented systems. However, on a larger scale, formal semantics of many well-known concepts are far from clear. For instance, there is no general consensus among researchers on the semantics of DAG-structured multiple inheritance networks with exceptions that commonly occur in knowledge representation contexts [Thirunarayan, 1995, Thirunarayan and Kifer, 1993, Touretzky et al., 1987]. This is partly because real-world node labels carry connotations that cannot be adequately reflected purely through the topology of the network. In fact, to quote Nelson Goodman (1955): *"The utility of a notion testifies not to its clarity, but rather to the philosophical importance of clarifying it."*

2.3.2 DESCRIPTIVE APPROACHES SUMMARY

Descriptive approaches try to capture contemporary usages of terms, to eventually promote consensus. In practice, the notion of equivalence is hard to formalize because it ranges from the well-grounded syntactic equality to various shades of similarity depending on domain and user-context.

Extensible Markup Language (XML) and XML Schema

Extensible Markup Language (XML) is a set of syntactic rules for encoding documents and data in a machine-readable form. It is a metalanguage for designing custom markup languages for different sorts of documents and data. Hypertext Markup Language (HTML) is an instance of XML. Even though originally HTML was intended to make the logical structure and content of a semi-structured document explicit, it evolved into a markup language for presentation. XML Schemas are analogous to context-free grammars in that they specify valid nested structures. XML tags are syntactic in nature and their presence simplifies parsing. For this reason, Web services use XML serialization as an information interchange format. There has also been exploratory work on developing XML-based programming languages [Plusch and Fry, 2003, Thirunarayan, 2005, Thirunarayan et al., 2005].

Entity-Relationship Model (ERM) and Unified Modelling Language (UML)

Entity-Relationship Model (ERM) is used to design a conceptual scheme or semantic data model of an information system. An entity represents an object (e.g., book, person). A relationship captures how two or more entities are related to one another (e.g., authorOf, causes). Entities and relationships can both have attributes (e.g., age, or totalCost [associated with an order for an item from a supplier]). Entities have primary keys, which are uniquely identifying attributes (e.g., studentId, SSN). Variants of ERMs provide additional notation for capturing weak relationship semantics such as cardinality constraints, participation constraints, generalization, and specialization.

The Unified Modeling Language (UML) is used to specify, visualize, modify, construct, and document an object-oriented software system (in contrast with databases or information systems), especially the structure and the behavior (including interaction) of system components, to varying degrees of detail.

Controlled Vocabulary, Thesaurus, and Taxonomy

Controlled vocabularies provide a way to organize knowledge by grouping together terms corresponding to a concept, and mandating the use of preferred/normalized terms to refer to the concept. For instance, controlled vocabularies are used for indexing and cataloging books in a library. They are used for formalizing materials and process specifications by defining terms for describing composition, processing, treatment, and testing of alloys, and packaging for shipment. Controlled vocabularies facilitate capturing and communicating semantics of a document through preferred terms, that is, enable determining semantic equivalence through syntactic matching of mapped preferred terms.

A thesaurus is similar to a controlled vocabulary in that it associates a term with a group of terms that are synonymous (share the same denotation) or very similar. According to Miller [1997], the thesaurus is a lexico-semantical[1] model of a conceptual reality or its constituent, which is expressed in the form of a system of terms and their (hierarchical and associative) relations, offers access via multiple aspects, and is used as a processing and searching tool of an information retrieval unit [Miller, 1997]. In the context of polysemous words, that is, words with multiple senses, the thesaurus provides groups of terms capturing different word senses. For instance, "deduct" can mean to take away (subtract, discount) or to infer (conclude, judge). Roget's Thesaurus for English language was created by Dr. Peter Mark Roget in 1805 and has been used by people at large as a ready reference. In general, theasuri are used extensively in information retrieval to improve recall by query expansion. WORDNET [Fellbaum, 1998] groups nouns, verbs, adjectives, and adverbs into sets of cognitive synonyms (synsets), and these sets are further organized using semantic relations such as broadening/generalization, narrowing/specialization, is-part-of, includes, and entailment. Synsets

---

[1]Lexical semantics concerned with the identification and representation of the semantics of lexical items.

can be used in equational reasoning while ISA-relationships can be used in inheritance reasoning. A thesaurus can be constructed manually by experts or mined automatically from a relevant corpus using co-occurrence statistics and context.

Taxonomy refers to hierarchical classification and nomenclature. Historically, Carl Linnaeus is credited with developing the first well-developed taxonomy to classify organisms. It used a binomial nomenclature system consisting of a generic name followed by a specific epithet to stand for a class of organism (e.g., Homo Sapiens for humans, Solanum Lycopersicum for tomatoes). The relationship between neighboring concepts in a taxonomy does not have a fixed interpretation, that is, it can represent generalization/specialization, whole-part, or some other association (e.g., Flynn's taxonomy classifies computer architectures as: SISD, SIMD, MISD, and MIMD, where S=Single, I=Instruction, M=Multiple, and D=Data.) Cloud taxonomy classifies services as: IaaS, PaaS, SaaS, and DaaS, where I=Infrastructure, P=Platform, S=Software, D=Data Analytics, and aaS=as a Service. ACM categories and subject descriptors provide taxonomy to classify a technical paper based on its content.

The Unified Medical Language System (UMLS) (http://www.nlm.nih.gov/research/umls/) is a widely used resource that integrates various controlled vocabularies using a biomedical thesaurus and taxonomy. It consists of a metathesaurus of medical concepts (obtained from established vocabularies such as SNOMED, ICD-9-CM, and MeSH) and inter-concept relationships to enable information exchange between different clinical databases and systems. That is, UMLS supports conversion of terms from one controlled medical vocabulary to another. UMLS also consists of a semantic network, which specifies categories (e.g., Disease or Syndrome, Biologic Function, Antibiotic) to which medical concepts (e.g., Adrenal Gland Disease, Adrenal Disorder, Surrenale Maladies [French]) defined in the Metathesaurus can belong, and semantic relationships (e.g., functionally related to, affected-by, temporally related to, follows, etc.) that can be assigned between these concepts. UMLS contains 135 semantic types and 54 semantic network relationships. See Figure 2.2 illustrating the concept Addison's disease and several terms (lexical manifestation) signifying it.

Folksonomy

Folksonomy is a taxonomy created by folks (ordinary users). It consists of freely selectable keywords or tags, which can be liberally attached to any information resource [Gruber, 2007]. The motivation for assigning tags to Web resources or entities is to succinctly summarize the nature or content or context of the information resource, such as photos, videos, and web pages. The tags provide multiple perspectives on a resource that facilitates sharing, organizing, and retrieving the resource (especially the multimedia kind). The tagging process is also referred to as social tagging, collaborative indexing, and social bookmarking. A folksonomy is very easy to create and use (compared to more formal approaches to semantics). However, it is prone to user subjectivity bias. Because the tag search is based on syntactic matching, its success relies on how well the tags reflect consensus between the categorization vocabulary used by the creators and the retrieval vocabulary used by the consumers. Thus, the search effectiveness is not guaranteed.

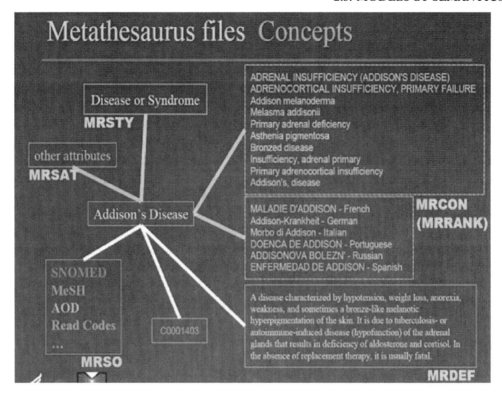

Figure 2.2: Concept Addison's Disease and its lexical manifestations [Bodenreider, 2007].

Folksonomy grew out of a bottom-up process of people tagging Web content they created or encountered (using applications such as social bookmarking [Del.icio.us] and social photo-sharing [Flickr]). In contrast, typical taxonomies are developed in a top-down manner [Peters, 2009]. Whereas taxonomies constrain the local choices at the leaves by global categorizations in the branches, folksonomies as practised do not impose such global consistency requirements. So, as Tom Gruber[2] observed, taxonomy is really an embodiment of top-down categorization as a way of finding and organizing information, while folksonomy is really the observation that we now have an entirely new source of data for finding and organizing information: user participation.

General Methods for Creation and Publication of Semantic Models

Descriptive semantic models can be constructed manually, semi-automatically, or automatically. For instance, UMLS is an example of a manually curated semantic model. On the other hand, DOOZER [Thomas, 2011] is a tool that has been used to semi-automatically create a semantic model (actually dynamic domain model) for human performance and cognition (HPC) domain by

[2]http://tomgruber.org/writing/ontology-of-folksonomy.htm

pruning a HPC-related taxonomy in Wikipedia and extending it with instance data extracted from PubMed. Similarly, VerbOcean is a broad-coverage semantic network of verbs semi-automatically mined from the Web documents [Chklovski and Pantel, 2004]. Fine-grained semantic relations between verbs such as similarity, antonymy, and temporal happens before relations between pairs of verbs are determined using lexico-syntactic patterns over the Web. Mitchell et al. [2009] discuss automatic extraction of structured information from unstructured text present on the Web.

Relationships are at the heart of semantic enrichment of documents and data. Historically, the theorem-proving community has made significant progress in the axiomatization, analysis, and implementation of reasoners for equality relationship [Plaisted, 1993]. Similarly, AI, databases, and the programming language communities have investigated the semantics of inheritance and tractability of inheritance reasoning [Lakshmanan and Thirunarayan, 1998]. The Semantic Web approach has enabled the use of annotations with a richer set of relationships to extract structured data from unstructured and semi-structured documents (as discussed in subsequent chapters), and use Linked Open Data (LOD) to serve as a repository of reusable structured data.

LOD (`http://linkeddata.org/`) provide an approach to publishing structured data (which includes ontologies and instance data) in a form that is conducive to their consumption. Berners Lee [2006] outlined four design principles of LOD:

1. Use URIs to identify things.

2. Use HTTP URIs so that these things can be referred to and looked up ("dereferenced") by people and user agents.

3. Provide useful information about the thing when the URI is dereferenced, using standard formats such as RDF/XML.

4. Include links to other, related URIs in the exposed data to improve discovery of other related information on the Web.

New techniques and tools are being developed for querying and question answering from large collections of linked data (containing medical knowledge, public government data, etc.) that can be used by non-computer specialists. This requires an ability to formulate questions over LOD for wider adoption, automatic techniques for aligning query vocabulary and the concepts and properties appearing in LOD datasets to enhance the quality and coverage of answers, and approaches for relevance ranking of LOD datasets and answer sets. Query interpretation involves novel application of symbolic information, statistical correlation, and relevance feedback. Specifically, Semantic Web technologies are being investigated to address outstanding challenges in the development of an intuitive notation for querying, robust techniques for ontology alignment, effective techniques for mapping natural language descriptions to LOD concepts, algorithms for constructing optimal overall query interpretations, and for generating executable formal queries.

To tap into rapidly growing, distributed LOD, ontology alignment systems have predominantly focused on variants of isA-relationship among concepts (e.g., rdfs:subclassOf, owl:equivalentClass, and owl:sameAs) [Jain et al., 2010, 2011]. However, it is also important to learn the isA-relationship among properties (e.g., rdfs:subPropertyOf) and other types of relationships among concepts (such as partonomy [Jain et al., 2009], causes [Gu, 2010], and other linguistic relations) for developing natural and expressive queries. Currently researchers are developing heuristics for inferring such relationships in the LOD context. Specifically, techniques based on (i) string-matching, (ii) domain and range specifications (signatures), and (iii) extensions matching are being explored. For instance, consider the following relationships from the DBPedia datasets.

Table 2.2: Sample DBPedia relationships		
Property	**Domain**	**Range**
isPartOf	Brain	AnatomicalStructure
parOfWineRegion	WineRegion	WineRegion
innervates	Nerve	AnatomincalStructure

In the first example, shown in Table 2.2 both the property name and the signature imply that it stands for a partonomy relation. In the second example, the substring matching "partof" can provide evidence of part-whole relationship, while the signature is not conclusive. In the third example, the property name is opaque but the signature provides evidence of part-whole relationship.

The ultimate goal of this line of research is to promote interoperability and reuse of machine-processable semantic models that are being created organically.

2.4   ONTOLOGY AND ONTOLOGY DEVELOPMENT

So far we have discussed different types of semantics, semantic models, and their applications. Now we bring together and summarize issues related to ontologies as is applicable to Semantic Web practice.

2.4.1   WHAT IS AN ONTOLOGY?

Gruber [1995] has given perhaps the most accepted definition of ontology as used in the context of information systems and the Web: "An ontology is an explicit specification of a conceptualization." The term is borrowed from philosophy, where an ontology is a systematic account of existence. For AI systems, what "exists" is what can be "represented." That is, ontologies are computational models that enable certain kinds of automated reasoning. According to Gruber [2008]: "In the context of computer and information sciences, an ontology defines a set of representational primitives with which to model a domain of knowledge or discourse. The definitions of the representational primitives include information about their meaning and constraints on their logically consistent application. Ontologies are typically specified in languages that allow one to abstract away the data structures and implementation strategies; in practice, the languages of ontologies are closer in expressive power to first-order logic than languages used to model databases. For this reason, ontologies are said to be at the 'semantic' level, whereas database schema are models of data at the 'logical' or 'physical' level."

According to Chandrasekaran et al. [1999], "Ontological analysis clarifies the structure of knowledge. Given a domain, its ontology forms the heart of any system of knowledge representation for that domain. Without ontologies, or the conceptualizations that underlie knowledge, there cannot be a vocabulary for representing knowledge. Second, ontologies enable knowledge sharing." A model/representation of the real world is relevant concepts, entities, attributes, relationships, domain vocabulary, and factual knowledge, all connected via a semantic network.

According to Guarino [1998], "An ontology is a logical theory accounting for the intended meaning of a formal vocabulary, i.e., its ontological commitment to a particular conceptualization of the world. The intended models of a logical language using such a vocabulary are constrained by its ontological commitment. An ontology indirectly reflects this commitment (and the underlying conceptualization) by approximating these intended models." The ontological commitment governs the use and meaning of the word, and as a consequence the applications' use of it. The ontology is language-dependent while the conceptualization is language-independent [Gustavsson, 2001]. In spite of differences in the vocabulary, it is possible to achieve interoperability between different ontologies if the conceptualization is the same because one can potentially develop mapping between related terms. In the context of Semantic Web, ontology languages provide specific formalisms for encoding domain knowledge to promote interoperability. It can serve as an *interface specification* for communicating with an agent. Ontology engineering is concerned with making representational choices that capture the relevant distinctions of a domain at the highest level of abstraction while still being as clear as possible about the meanings of terms [Gruber, 2003].

For our purpose, an *ontology* consists of ontology schema and its associated knowledge base consisting of factual information represented as instances of classes and relationships (also called assertions). A *populated ontology* is an ontology schema with associated knowledge base. Ontology schema is a formal explicit description of concepts in a domain of discourse (*classes*), properties of each concept describing various features and attributes of the concept, and relationship among concepts (*attributes* and *relationships*). Unless explicitly specified otherwise, we will use the term ontology to mean populated ontology.

Two important characteristics of an ontology follows:

- Ontologies represent agreement within a domain of discourse. This is called *ontology commitment*. The scope of ontological commitment may be a community of users, workgroup, enterprise, industry, or beyond. Unless an existing ontology or metadata standard is used to bootstrap an ontology, it is desirable to choose the largest possible scope for ontological commitment. Sometimes, ontology schema is based on an existing industry metadata standard in which case it is the scope of the metadata standard which determines the scope.

- An ontology typically provides a terminological agreement or a support for nomenclature which allow for better resolution of terminological differences (i.e., naming heterogeneity). At the minimum, this involves support for synonyms, but may also involve homonym and other linguistic relationships.

Classes describe concepts in the domain and are the focus of most ontologies. A class can have *subclasses* that represent concepts that are more specific than the superclass. In practical terms, developing an ontology schema includes [Noy and McGuinness, 2001]:

- Defining classes in the ontology;

- Arranging the classes in a taxonomic (subclass—superclass) hierarchy; and

- Defining attributes/relationships and describing allowed values for these.

2.4.2   HOW DO WE DEVELOP AN ONTOLOGY?

We discuss general issues to consider while constructing ontologies. An ontology is an artifact that is designed for a purpose, which is to enable the modeling of knowledge about some domain, real or imagined [Gruber, 2008]. There are always viable alternatives to model a domain, and as such, the application that would use the ontology and anticipated extensions should be the driving factors for the best solution. As a general rule, concepts in the ontology should be close to physical or logical objects and relationships in the domain of interest [Noy and McGuinness, 2001]. Essentially, an ontology defines the concepts, relationships, and other distinctions by providing meanings for the representational vocabulary and formal constraints on its coherent use [Gruber, 2008]. The nouns used while describing the domain are most likely to be modeled as classes, and verbs used are most likely to be modeled as relationships. One should start developing the ontology by defining its domain and scope. The main questions to be asked to determine the scope should include:

- What are we going to use the ontology for? Often an ontology of the domain is not a goal in itself. Developing an ontology is akin to defining a set of data and their structure for other programs to use [Noy and McGuinness, 2001]. Applications use ontologies and knowledge bases built from ontologies as data.

- Which types of questions should the ontology help provide answers for? These are sometimes referred to as **competency questions** [Gruninger and Fox, 1995]. Does the ontology contain enough information to answer these types of questions? Do the answers require a particular level of detail or representation of a particular area? These competency questions are just a sketch and do not need to be exhaustive [Noy and McGuinness, 2001]. For example, assuming we are developing an ontology about research and researchers, questions like: "How has a certain tool been used to provide support to one another?," "What kind of research activities may lead to certain results?," "Who has been involved in what activities and is therefore capable of conducting what activities?," and "Who are the researchers citing Researcher A's certain publication?," are posed.

- Which knowledge sources are available to populate the knowledge base? What kind of information do these data sources provide? Note that structurally, the knowledge sources may be any traditional data repository or representation, including relational databases, XML and HTML documents, and spreadsheets.

In addition to competency questions, it is useful to write down a list of all terms we would like either to make statements about or to explain to a user [Noy and McGuinness, 2001]. In the case of research domains, these terms may include author, publication, researcher, conference, publication date, place, author, researcher's affiliation, books, and where a conference takes place. The terms that describe objects having independent existence, as opposed to describing other objects, should be modeled as classes in the ontology. The classes should then be organized into a hierarchical taxonomy. If being an instance of one class necessitates being an instance of some other class, then these two classes should be defined as sub/super classes respectively. For example: consider Faculty vs. Person. One cannot be a faculty member without being a Person. In this case, Faculty should be defined as a subclass of Person.

There are several possible approaches to developing a class hierarchy [Uschold and Gruninger, 1996]:

- *Top-down approach*: Start with the most general concepts in the domain and then specialize the concepts. There is a danger of starting with too few general concepts, risking imprecision and rework.

- *Bottom-up approach*: Start with the leaves of the hierarchy (most specific classes) and then generalize them to create upper-level classes. One would be required to start with a large set of specific classes, risking that they may not be usable/important for the final ontology.

- *Middle-out approach*: Define the most salient, basic concepts first before defining super and sub-ordinate ones. This approach strikes a balance in the level of detail. Details are added when it is necessary by specializing the basic concepts. In our example domain, we may start with "publication" and "researcher" for example and then specialize into "journal," or "magazine," etc., and generalize to "Person" as deemed necessary.

The classes alone will not provide enough information to answer the competency questions. Most of the remaining terms (i.e., terms not used to define classes) are likely to be properties of these classes (like location of the conference, date of the publication). After deciding which class each property describes, the properties become attributes/relationships attached to those classes. As a rule of thumb, verbs are modeled as relationships and modifiers or "refiners"—roughly adjectives and adverbs in ordinary language are modeled as attributes. This decision, though, is not always straightforward. It is tightly coupled with the selection of classes (what to model as "self-standing entities," see below).

We now describe some of the heuristics/guidelines to use while making modeling choices.

2.4.3   CLASS VS. PROPERTY (ATTRIBUTE/RELATIONSHIP)

The following classification may help in deciding whether the term should be modeled as a "self-standing entity" (class) or through properties.

- Sortal: (Roughly) the nouns in natural language. According to Jones et al. [1998], a sortal predicate (like apple) "supplies a principle for distinguishing and counting individual particulars which it collects." It is further refined into:

    - Substantial: corresponding to types, like person

    - Non-substantial: corresponding to roles, like student

- Non-sortal: (Roughly) adjectives and verbs in natural language. A non-sortal predicate (like red) "supplies such a principle only for particulars already distinguished, or distinguishable, in accordance with some antecedent principle or method" [Guarino et al., 1994].

Normally, sortal predicates should become self-standing entities and non-sortal predicates should be attached to those as attributes or relationships. However, one should not use the above classification alone to determine the classes in the ontology. Sometimes, it may be necessary to introduce a new class (like Red Apple) rather than representing the distinction through different property values (hasColor relationship to a "Color" class, or "Color" attribute). It is hard to navigate both an extremely nested hierarchy with many extraneous classes and a very flat hierarchy that has too few classes with too much information encoded in properties. Finding the appropriate balance though is not easy [Noy and McGuinness, 2001]. One should take the visualization aspects of the hierarchy into account as well.

There are several rules of thumb that help decide when to introduce new classes in a hierarchy [Noy and McGuinness, 2001]:

- Subclasses of a class usually (a) have additional properties that the superclass does not have, or (b) participate in different relationships than the super classes.

- Classes in terminological hierarchies do not have to introduce new properties.

- If the concepts with different attribute values become restrictions for different properties in other classes, then we should create a new class for the distinction. Otherwise, we represent the distinction in an attribute value. For example, do we create a class "periodical publication" or do we simply create a class "publication" and attach property "type" and fill values like "serial," "periodical," "single," and so on? The answer depends on the scope of the ontology. If the concept of being periodic does not have any implications for its relations to other objects, then "periodical publication" should not be introduced as a class. But if in our domain periodical publication would have different subclasses such as "newspaper," "journal," "magazine" that we need to distinguish it, we should introduce "periodical publication" as a separate class.

- If a distinction is important in the domain and we think of the objects with different values for the distinction as different kinds of objects, then we should create a new class for the distinction. Consider the human-anatomy ontology given by Noy and McGuinness [2001]: When we represent ribs, do we create a class for each of the "1stleft rib," "2ndleft rib," and so on? Or do we have a class Rib with attributes for the order and the lateral position (left-right)? If the information about each of the ribs that we represent in the ontology is significantly different, then we should indeed create a class for each of the ribs. That is, if we want to represent detailed adjacency and location information (which is different for each rib) as well as specific functions that each rib plays and organs it protects, we want to represent each rib as a class. If we are modeling anatomy at a slightly lesser level of generality, and all ribs are very similar as far as our potential applications are concerned (e.g., we just want to talk about which rib is broken on the X-Ray without implications for other parts of the body), we may want to simplify our hierarchy and have just the class Rib, with two attributes: lateral position and order.

- Whenever we decide to model the distinction through properties rather than introducing a new class, we should once again apply the above rules to determine whether that property needs to be a relationship or an attribute. For example, if we decide to have "Color" as property rather than having "Red Apple," should we introduce a new class "Color" with instances "red," "blue," etc. and use a relationship "hasColor" or an attribute "color" with literals "red," "blue," and so on? In fact, similar modeling issues arise in the context of object-oriented software construction when we need to decide if a concept should be a subclass of another concept or should be a component of another concept, as explained in Meyer [1997]. For instance, class CarOwner does not multiply inherit from classes Car and Person, but rather singly inherits from Person but has an attribute named Car. The confusion is exacerbated by the fact that inheritance can be approximated using composition and delegation.

2.4.4   CLASS VS. INSTANCE

This decision heavily depends on the potential application of the ontology. One needs to determine the lowest level of granularity in the representation and these should become instances. If the most specific item to be represented in the knowledge base, for example, is the individual researcher, "researcher" should be the class and the individuals are the instances. Another thing to consider is that the instances cannot have sub-instances, only classes can be arranged in a hierarchy. Therefore, if there is a natural hierarchy among terms, such as in terminological hierarchies, we should define these terms as classes even though they may not have any instances of their own.

2.5   A WORD ABOUT PRACTICE

According to a recent survey about the types of knowledge models being used in practice, lightweight models seem to have an edge over more formal ontologies, at this time. Specifically, taxonomies are the favorite, as 73.6% of participants use or plan to use lightweight ontologies [Giunchiglia and Zaihrayeu, 2007], followed by thesauri (62%) and ontologies (61.2%), while simple glossaries lag considerably behind with a usage of 31.4%.[3] Figure 2.3 concisely summarizes the expressivity-tractability tradeoff discussed earlier.

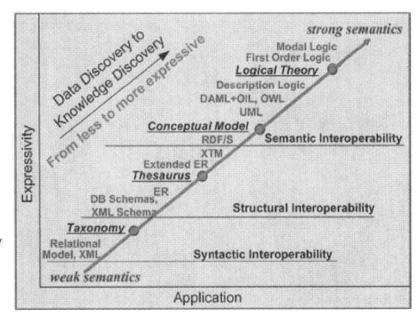

Figure 2.3: Expressivity-Tractability Tradeoff: Multiple levels of semantics and associated interoperability capabilities. Increasing interoperability services requires increasing community agreement [Obrst, 2003]

[3]http://blog.semantic-web.at/2011/05/11/which-kind-of-controlled-vocabularies-matter/

CHAPTER 3

Annotation—Adding Semantics to Data

In order to make any data (temperature, location, etc.), Web resource (image, audio file, video stream, etc.), or real-world entity (painting, IP camera, can of milk, airline reservation, etc.), collectively abbreviated as *objects*, machine understandable, we need to describe their characteristics/associated information in a machine processable manner. This requires determining what aspects of the objects to abstract and describe, *the semantic modeling problem*, and how to materialize these descriptions in a machine processable form that can elicit semantic comprehension and facilitate interoperability, *the representation and reasoning problem*. For instance, a photograph can be characterized by a variety of attributes including its subject, content, camera used, photographer, size, resolution, location, and time. One scalable and flexible way to achieve this is to associate metadata with an object (in the form of attribute-value pairs, for example) using standard, well-established terminology that can be reasoned with. In the Semantic Web approach, the former, that links syntax with its semantics, leads to different approaches to annotation such as RDFa and microdata, while the latter, that provides standard terminology and semantic machinery, leads to different ontologies, logical formalisms, and reasoners such as RDF/RDFS and OWL2.

The metadata that can be associated with an object can span a wide variety of characteristics. For instance, the metadata associated with multimedia content have been classified as [Klas and Sheth, 1998]:

- *Media type-specific metadata*: Attributes can be determined by the type of media, e.g., font size of text, frequencies in audio, speaker characteristics, camera tilt, and motion.

- *Media processing-specific metadata*: Attributes can be determined by the functions used to process a media, e.g., filtering information, delivery format, and byte transfer rate.

- *Content-specific metadata*: Attributes can be determined by the subject matter, e.g., time, location, and people in a photograph; event captured by a video; details of composition, composer and singer of a song; and title of a document.

Metadata can also be classified as content-dependent which includes theme/topic specific information, or content-independent which includes author/source/provenance specific information.

In this chapter, we discuss different forms of data and the nature of semantics to be gleaned from them. We then discuss approaches to make this semantics explicit [Uren et al., 2006]. Later, we also show how some of these techniques can be adapted to describe the semantics of Web services.

3.1   DIFFERENT FORMS OF DATA AND THEIR SEMANTICS

3.1.1   UNSTRUCTURED DATA

Unstructured data are normally text data that do not have any predefined structure imposed on their content. Such data can be further categorized as (i) grammatical text or (ii) user-generated content.

Grammatical Text

Grammatical text is exemplified by articles appearing in newspapers (such as those in The Wall Street Journal, or The New York Times), research journals (such as those in PubMed), magazines, and books. The text is characterized by the use of full sentences satisfying grammatical constraints. Automatic abstraction and assimilation of content can benefit from linguistic (syntactic and semantic) structure as well as domain-semantics provided by background knowledge (e.g., in bioinformatics/medical, economics, and technology). In fact, the seven DARPA-sponsored Message Understanding Conferences (MUC) over the period 1987-1997, and the more recent Text Retrieval Conferences (TREC) that began in the 1990s, have provided tremendous impetus for light-weight natural language processing for information extraction and retrieval from grammatical texts such as those involving terrorist events, corporate management succession events, and chemistry. All this has now culminated in the development of UIMA (Unstructured Information Management Architecture) that provides a common framework for content analytics (specifically, processing information to extract meaning and create structured data) [Apache, 2012].

Information extraction from grammatical text led to learning and use of syntactic patterns and contexts to recognize entity types (such as person, place, currency, and date) and relationships, use of semantic equivalences (such as via active and passive voice forms) to recognize the subject and the object of an "asymmetric" binary relation (especially in situations where the entity type is unable to disambiguate them, such as in X was victimized by Y, X replaced Y, and Y replaces X), and co-reference resolution techniques (including use of background knowledge in the form of aliases, acronyms, and synonyms).

User-Generated Content

User-generated content is exemplified by citizen sensor data/microblogs (such as from Twitter) and exchanges on social media (such as on Facebook). (Even though blogs fall under UGC, their structure is closer to grammatical text than the text found on Twitter and Facebook, so they are excluded.) The UGC text is characterized by being terse, colloquial, context-poor, and containing words/phrases with nonstandard/creative, homophone-based spellings. Automatic assimilation of content requires background knowledge (in the form of ontologies) to deal with implicit spatio-temporal-thematic context, and novel techniques and tools to summarize and visualize aggregated content to deal with its large size and real-time nature. Robust, scalable, and high-quality analysis of user-generated content is an active area of contemporary research. To improve scalability, one can exploit cloud computing infrastructure and data parallelism induced by partitioning data using spatio-temporal coordinates, and to improve the quality of analysis, one can exploit appropriate language models, scoring metrics, and thematic background knowledge, as discussed in later chapters.

3.1.2   SEMI-STRUCTURED DATA

Semi-structured data are normally text data that contain tags or other markers to delimit and capture hierarchical and aggregation structure associated with semantic fields within the data. HTML documents[1] and XML documents with domain-specific tags (such as DBLP XML records) are classic examples of semi-structured data. Recall that XML (eXtensible Markup Language) is a meta-language for designing customized markup languages for different document types and HTML is an XML application that specifies a particular set of tags for capturing organizational and presentation aspects of a text document. Typically, an XML document consists of tagged text (that is, markup inter-twined with text) in which the tag makes explicit the category and the properties of the enclosed text using attribute-value pairs. Even though the tags in semi-structured data are syntactic in nature, they are conducive to incorporating semantics in that the tags can be chosen from a standard semantic model or potentially mapped to one. For example, the tags can be display-oriented providing information such as color and font, or semantics-oriented providing information such as type and normal-form. Semantic tags permit abstraction of meaning in a standard form. In summary, semi-structured documents can contain descriptive text that is human comprehensible and semantic tags that are machine processable.

3.1.3   STRUCTURED DATA

Structured data have well-defined formal syntax and an associated data model. Relational databases, machine sensor data stream (such as from sensors on a weather station), RDF triples, and XML serialization of a Web-service call (for data interchange) all illustrate the variety in structured data. By definition, structured data can be parsed with relative ease. To provide semantics, we need to associate real-world objects/entities and their relationships with the structured data on the basis of their schema. To comprehend machine sensor data, it is also necessary to incorporate spatio-temporal-thematic context using information about time of measurement, location, and type of sensor, physical quantity measured, unit of measure, etc.

3.1.4   MULTIMEDIA DATA

We lump all other non-textual content together as multimedia data, which includes photos, videos, and audio clips found on social-media sharing services such as Flickr and YouTube. Due to the difficulties involved in analyzing multimedia content, the only viable approach to gleaning semantics is through the analysis of associated textual descriptors (metadata) and community comments.

---

[1]XML annotations can be applied (i) to text documents to impose additional syntactic and semantic structure on them to obtain semi-structured data, and (ii) to raw structured data with primitive values to obtain more expressive structured data. Examples of the former are the XHTML documents, and examples of the latter are the DBLP bibliographic records.

3.2   ROLE OF SEMANTIC METADATA

Semantic metadata describe contextually relevant, domain-specific information about content based on a custom (e.g., industry-specific or enterprise-specific) metadata model or ontology or information about its provenance. For example, if the content is from the business domain, the relevant semantic metadata could be company name, ticker symbol, industry sector, executives, etc., whereas if the content is from the intelligence domain, the relevant semantic metadata could be terrorist name, event, location, organization, etc. In contrast, syntactic metadata focus on elements such as size of the document, location of a document, or date of document creation. The provenance metadata can include information such as author, sensor, or processing details.

Software tools that analyze content by leveraging syntactic search, and even syntactic metadata, are inadequate for information integration. By developing and annotating documents with semantic metadata, software programs can automatically understand the full context of what each document means by relating various pieces of information present in the document, and enable the program to make the right decisions about why and how these documents should be combined or used.

An important characteristic of semantic metadata is that they include named relationships (such as "competes with," "is CEO of," etc); traditional statistical and concurrence analysis usually lead only to unnamed relationships. Such named relationships tell us why entities are related, enabling more automation and deeper insight. Expert domain agents can further enhance the extracted entities with semantically associated entities from an ontology. For example, on the basis of references to specific company names such as HPQ, HD, MSFT, ORCL, APPL, etc. in a document, one can go on to infer additional facts such as HPQ and HD are traded on the NYSE and MSFT, ORCL and APPL are components of the NASDAQ 100 Index.

The ontologies enable identification of "indirect relationships." The use of semantic associations [Anyanwu and Sheth, 2002, Sheth et al., 2004] allows entities not explicitly mentioned in the text to be inferred or linked to a document by incorporating such associated entities in the tagging of the document. The relationships that are retained are application specific and completely customizable, and their inclusion makes it possible to traverse "relationship chains" to more than one level from within the document. *This sort of exploitation of semantics is the tipping point favoring semantic technologies used to harness background domain knowledge for automatic unravelling of implicit relationships.*

Semantics not only provides a means to data reuse by normalization but also serves as a foundation for interchange formats to preserve existing investments in software infrastructure and to improve agility. Further, ontologies not only facilitate machine interpretation and communication, they also provide useful labels and documentation for human consumption.

Semantic metadata are useful because they are derived using appropriate domain-specific contexts. For instance, if there was an insignificant reference to President of United States as a guest at a friend's party, then extraction of President's name as a politician is not of much value, because the name is not contextually relevant semantic metadata. On the other hand, if it were in the context of a political fund raiser, politics-specific semantic metadata elements can accurately serve as descriptors of the overall content. In other words, the domain-specificity of semantic metadata elements is essential to establishing the right context and relevance.

3.3   APPROACHES TO ADDING SEMANTICS TO DATA

XML annotation of a text document enables syntactic level interoperability. To explore semantic level interoperability, one can develop suitable ontologies and annotation frameworks for adding semantic metadata. For example, in the context of sensor data interpretation, one can develop ontologies for describing sensors and sensor data, and techniques for associating the ontology concepts with sensor data. In what follows, we discuss approaches to adding semantics to different forms of data by embedding semantic tags or mapping tags to an ontology (semantic model). We use the terms tags/tagging synonymously with the terms annotations/annotating.

3.3.1   MICROFORMATS

A microformat is an approach to semantic markup that seeks to reuse existing HTML/XHTML tags to incorporate metadata. Specifically, it embeds and encodes semantics within the attributes of markup tags. This approach allows contact information, geographic coordinates, and calendar events, etc., to be both human readable and machine processable (using hCard, geo, and hCalendar microformats respectively) as illustrated below.

The text: "Dayton, OH is located at 39.59, -84.22." can be annotated using geo-microformat as:

```
Dayton, OH is located at
<span class="geo">
   <span class="latitude">39.59</span>,
   <span class="longitude">-84.22</span>
</span>
```

The HTML fragment

```
<div>
   <div>Amit Sheth</div>
   <div>Kno.e.sis Center</div>    <div>937-775-5217</div>
   <a href="http://knoesis.org/">http://knoesis.org/</a>
</div>
```

can be semantically enhanced using the hCard microformat markup as

```
<div class=card">
   <div class="fn">Amit Sheth</div>
   <div class="org">Kno.e.sis Center</div>
   <div class="tel">937-775-5217</div>
   <a class="url" href="http://knoesis.org/">http://knoesis.org/</a>
</div>
```

The class attribute values fn, org, tel, and url stand for formatted name, organization, telephone number, and Uniform Resource Locator respectively. hCard is an HTML version of the vCard standard. XLink (XML Linking Language) is an XML markup language for creating hyperlinks in XML documents.

3.3.2   XLINK AND MODEL REFERENCE

XLink also outlines methods for describing links between resources in XML documents. Any element in an XML document can behave as a target of a link. For example, XLink attributes can be added to SensorML and Observation and Measurement (O&M) documents to semantically annotate sensor data. A link between a sensor datum and its semantic model is a *model reference*. XLink supports simple links (such as in HTML) and extended links (for linking multiple resources together such as forming a complete graph of a set of elements). In addition, the links can be defined externally to the linked files, and typically extended links are stored separately from the resources they associate.

The following example illustrates a Sensor Observation Service (SOS) GetCapabilities document describing a service for a weather station. The sensor description is semantically annotated with model references to classes and individuals related to a sensor, observed properties, and a location (Xlink-SSW). This GetCapabilities response says that the sensor "WeatherStation_1" located at the point (18.556825, -72.297935) can observe "snow-precipitation," "temperature," and "windspeed."

```
<?xml version ="1.0" encoding = ''UTF–8"?>
<sos : Contents >
 <sos : ObservationOfferingList >
  <sos : ObservationOffering
      gml : id = ''urn : ogc : def : procedure :JPEO–CBD:: WeatherStation_1">

   <gml : name> urn : ogc : def : procedure :JPEO–CBD:: WeatherStation_1 </gml : name>
     <gml : boundedBy>
       <gml : Envelope  srsName ="urn : ogc : def : crs :EPSG:4326">
          <gml : lowerCorner >18.556825  −72.297935</gml : lowerCorner >
          <gml : upperCorner >18.556825  −72.297935</gml : upperCorner >
       </gml : Envelope >
       </gml : boundedBy>
     <sos : time >           <gml : TimeInstant  xsi : type ="gml : TimeInstantType">
          <gml : timePosition  indeterminate = ''now"/>
          </gml : TimeInstant >
     </sos : time >
     <sos : procedure
xlink : href="http :// purl . oclc . org/NET/ ssnx/ ssn–dev#WeatherStation_1"/>
     <sos : observedProperty
xlink : href="http :// purl . oclc . org/NET/ ssnx/ cf/ cf–property#snow–precipitatio
n"/>
     <sos : observedProperty
xlink : href="http :// purl . oclc . org/NET/ ssnx/ cf/ cf–property#temperature"/>
     <sos : observedProperty
xlink : href="http :// purl . oclc . org/NET/ ssnx/ cf/ cf–property#windspeed"/>
     <sos : featureOfInterest  xlink : href ="http ://sws . geonames . org/5248611/"/>
     <sos : responseFormat > text/xml; subtype ="om/1.0.0 </sos : responseFormat >
     <sos : resultModel
xmlns : ns ="http ://www. opengis . net/om/1.0">ns : Observation </sos : resultModel >
     <sos : responseMode > inline </sos : responseMode >
```

```
<sos : responseMode > resultTemplate </sos : responseMode >
</sos : ObservationOffering >
</sos : ObservationOfferingList >
</sos : Contents >
```

An important benefit of semantically annotating sensor data is the additional expressiveness supplied by an ontological representation. For example, if a weather ontology defines winter storms and their observable properties, then annotating sensor data with concepts from this ontology enables the ability to reason over such concepts. From observations generated by this weather station, a blizzard may be inferred and a suitable sos:featureOfInterest tag, which links to a blizzard individual, can be added.

	Table 3.1: Mapping XLink to RDF	
Attribute	**Description**	**Intended RDF**
xlink:href	Identifier of the resource which is the target of the association, given as a URI	rdf:about of range resource
xlink:role	Nature of the target resource, given as a URI	rdf:about of class of range resource
xlink:arcrole	Role or purpose of the target resource in relation to the present resource, given as a URI	rdf:about of object property linking domain element to range resource
xlink:title	Text describing the association or the target resource	rdfs:comment

The following example illustrates an observation with sensor `rain_gauge_sth_esk_up_esk_rd_bridge` that measures *thickness_of_rainfall_amount*.

```
<swes : offering  xlink : role ="http :// purl . oclc . org /NET/ ssnx / ssn # Observation "
    xlink : arcrole ="http ://www. loa−cnr . it / ontologies /DUL. owl# hasSetting >
  <sos : ObservationOffering >
    <swes : procedureIdentifier
        xlink : role ="http :// purl . oclc . org /NET/ ssnx / ssn # SensingDevice "
        xlink : href ="http :// purl . oclc . org /NET/ ssnx / ssndev #
            rain_gauge_sth_esk_up_esk_rd_bridge "
        xlink : arcrole ="http :// purl . oclc . org /NET/ ssnx / ssn # observedBy ">
      http :// csiro . au/ sw/ rain_gauge_sth_esk_up_esk_rd_bridge
    </swes : procedureIdentifier >

    <swes : observableProperty
    xlink : href ="http :// purl . oclc . org /NET/ ssnx / cf / cfproperty #
        thickness_of_rainfall_amount "

    xlink : arcrole ="http :// purl . oclc . org /NET/ ssnx / ssn # observedProperty "
    xlink : role ="http :// purl . oclc . org /NET/ ssnx / qu/ dim# Distance "/>
      <sos : phenomenonTime
        xlink : role ="http ://www.w3. org /2006/ time−entry # Interval ">
```

```
        xlink:arcrole="http://purl.oclc.org/NET/ssnx/ssn#observationTime"
    <gml:TimePeriod gml:id="phenomenonTime11">
    <gml:beginPosition
        xlink:role="http://www.w3.org/2006/time-entry#begins"
        xlink:arcrole="http://www.w3.org/2001/XMLSchema#time">
      2001-01-11T16:22:25.00
    </gml:beginPosition>
      <gml:endPosition
        xlink:role="http://www.w3.org/2006/time-entry#ends"
        xlink:arcrole="http://www.w3.org/2001/XMLSchema#time">
      2005-10-18T19:54:13.000Z
      </gml:endPosition>
    </gml:TimePeriod>
    </sos:phenomenonTime>
  </sos:ObservationOffering>
</swes:offering>
```

This example encodes information that the observation of *thickness_of_rainfall_amount*, a Distance, is being observed by *rain_gauge_sth_esk_up_esk_rd_bridge*, a SensingDevice, over a time interval. Specifically, xlink:href formalizes the object URL, xlink:role captures class/type information associated with an object, and xlink:arcrole captures relation/property information between two objects.

3.3.3   RDFA

RDFa (Resource Description Framework - in - attributes) adds a set of attribute-level extensions to XHTML for embedding rich metadata within Web documents [Hausenblas et al., 2008, Hickson, 2011]. RDFa is a W3C-proposed standard[2] and a markup language that enables the layering of RDF information on any XHTML or XML document. RDFa provides a set of attributes that can represent semantic metadata within an XML language from which RDF triples can be extracted using simple mapping. The core subset of RDFa attributes[3] include

- *about*—a URI extracted as the subject of an RDF triple that specifies the resource the metadata is about;

- *rel* and *rev*—extracted as the object property (predicate) of an RDF triple, this URI specifies a relationship or reverse-relationship with another resource;

- *href, src,* and *resource*—extracted as the object of an RDF triple, this URI specifies the partner resource;

- *property*—extracted as the datatype property (predicate) of an RDF triple, this URI specifies a property for the content of an element; and

[2]http://www.w3.org/2006/07/SWD/RDFa/
[3]http://en.wikipedia.org/wiki/RDFa

- *instanceof*—extracted as the object property "rdf:type" coupled with an RDF triple's object, this optional attribute specifies the RDF type of the subject (the resource that the metadata is about).

The RDF data model mapping enables its use for embedding RDF triples within XHTML documents in a form suitable for extraction of RDF triples by compliant user agents. Use of RDFa improves traceability and minimizes duplication of information in comparison with an approach that maintains a separate translation/abstraction of a document into RDF. For example, RDFa attributes can be added to SensorML and O&M documents to provide semantic annotations of the sensor data, and for extracting equivalent RDF triples from them (see Chapter 6, Section 6.3.1).

```
<div prefix="og: http://ogp.me/ns# dc: http://purl.org/dc/elements/1.1/" about="/
    photos">
    <h2 property="og:title">Hubble Space Telescope's Top Images</h2>
    Sombrero Galaxy (M104) is an edge-on spiral galaxy, 50,000 light-years across
        and 28 million light years from Earth.
    <div about="http://example.com/photos/sombrero.jpg">
        <img src="http://example.com/photos/sombrero.jpg" />
        <span property="dc:title">The Majestic Sombrero Galaxy (M104)
        </span>
        <span property="dc:creator">Hubble Space Telescope
        </span>
    </div>
</div>
```

The above RDFa example shows use of Open Graph Protocol and Dublin Core vocabularies (including an association of a title and a creator to an image). In general, the Open Graph protocol enables any web page to become a rich object in a social graph by specifying metadata terms such as title, type, image, and URL, and the Dublin Core specifies metadata terms to describe Web and physical resources such as title, creator, publisher, and date [Facebook, 2011]. The resulting extracted RDF triples are shown below.

```
<http://example.com/photos>
    <http://ogp.me/ns#title> "The Majestic Sombrero Galaxy (M104)"

<http://example.com/photos/sombrero.jpg>
    <http://purl.org/dc/elements/1.1/title>"The Majestic Sombrero Galaxy (M104)"

<http://example.com/photos/sombrero.jpg>
    <http://purl.org/dc/elements/1.1/creator> "Hubble Space Telescope"
```

Table 3.3 provides a comparison of the capabilities of XLink and RDFa to express types defined in RDF. In this respect, as the table demonstrates, RDFa is more expressive than XLink.

Microformats vs. RDFa: Superficially, both microformats and RDFa have similar goals—embed semantic markup for machine processing (such as for providing rich snippets in Search Engine Results Page [SERP]) while simultaneously reusing content for human readability. However, they differ in their development philosophies in that microformats is a grassroots developers' effort to address immediate semantic integration problems, while RDFa is focused on designing a standards-

Attribute	Description	Intended RDF
Table 3.2: Mapping RDFa to RDF		
rdfa:about	The identification of the resource (to state what the datum is about)	rdf:about of domain resource
rdfa:typeof	RDF type(s) to associate with a resource	rdf:about of class of a resource
rdfa:href	Partner resource of a relationship ('resource object')	rdf:about of range resource
rdfa:property	Relationship between a subject and some literal text ('predicate')	rdf:about of datatype property
rdfa:rel	Relationship between two resources ('predicate')	rdf:about of object property
rdfa:rev	Reverse relationship between two resources ('predicate')	rdf:about of (inverse) object property
rdfa:src	Base resource of a relationship when the resource is embedded ('resource object')	rdf:about of domain resource
rdfa:resource	Partner resource of a relationship that is not intended to be 'clickable' ('object')	rdf:about of range resource
rdfa:datatype	Datatype of a property	XML type range of datatype property
rdfa:content	Machine-readable content ('plain literal object')	Value for datatype property

based, scalable solution of lasting value. Even though, currently, microformats are a de facto standard, while RDFa is a de jure standard, it is hoped that both communities will converge to a mutually acceptable annotation framework.

3.3.4 MICRODATA

Microdata are an HTML5 specification used to embed semantics within Web documents. It is an attempt to provide a simpler alternative to approaches such as RDFa and Microformats for annotating HTML elements, to enable applications such as search engines and Web crawlers to better assimilate web page content. The following illustration of microdata annotations and the corresponding property-value pairs is about an instance of type "http://example.org/animals#cat" [Hickson, 2011]. (See also Table 3.4.)

```
<section itemscope itemtype="http://example.org/animals#cat">
        <h1 itemprop="name http://example.com/fn">Hedral</h1>
        <p itemprop="desc">Hedral is a male american domestic shorthair, with a fluffy
<span   itemprop="http://example.com/color">black</span> fur with
<span itemprop="http://example.com/color">white</span> paws and belly. </p>
        <img itemprop="img" src="hedral.jpeg" alt="" title="Hedral, age 18 months"> </
        section>
```

Table 3.3: Comparison of XLink and RDFa

RDF Mapping	XLink	RDFa
Domain Instance		rdfa:about or rdfa:src
Domain Class	xlink:role	rdfa:typeof
Object Property	xlink:arcrole	rdfa:rel
Inverse Object Property		rdfa:rev
Range Instance Object Property	xlink:href	rdfa:href or rdfa:resource
Range Class	Model Reference	rdfa:typeof
Datatype Property	Microformat	rdfa:property
Range Value	RDFa	rdfa:content or element content

Table 3.4: What is my name?

Property	Value
name	Hedral
http://example.com/fn	Hedral
desc	Hedral is a male american domestic shorthair, with a fluffy black fur with white paws and belly.
http://example.com/color	black
http://example.com/color	white
img	.../hedral.jpeg

Hickson et al. [2012] describe processing rules that may be used to extract RDF from an HTML document containing microdata.

3.3.5 SA-REST: SEMANTICALLY ENHANCING RESTFUL SERVICES AND RESOURCES

Semantic Annotations for REST (SA-REST) is a way to augment semantic class names as additional metadata to Web resources and REST API descriptions [Fielding, 2000, Zuzak, 2010] in HTML or XHTML. (REST is discussed in more detail in Chapter 5.) In fact, any resource can be viewed as a service. The metadata can come from various semantic models such an ontology, taxonomy, or a tag cloud. The embedded metadata permit various enhancements, such as improving search, facilitating data mediation, easing services integration, and enabling smart mashups.

SA-REST[4] defines three basic properties that can be used to unobtrusively annotate HTML/XHTML documents. That is, it reuses existing XHTML constructs and caters to both humans and machines. The properties, domain-rel, sem-rel, and sem-class are specified using the class at-

---

[4]http://www.w3.org/Submission/SA-REST/

tribute and the title attribute defined by the HTML4 specification. Similar to microformats, the scope of the annotation is defined by the HTML element that bears the annotation.

1. **domain-rel**: This property allows a domain information description of a resource. If a given resource has content spanning multiple domains, it may be necessary to add multiple domain-rel property entries, each corresponding to a section of the resource. If such a separation cannot be made, then the resource may be attached with an enumeration of values as the domain-rel property value.

2. **sem-rel**: The sem-rel property captures the semantics of a link, and evolves from the popular rel tag. This property enables the addition of externalized annotations to third party documents. A sem-rel property may only be used with an anchor (`<a>`) element.

3. **sem-class**: This property can be used to markup a single entity within a resource. The entity may be a term, a text fragment, or embedded objects such as a video.

The following example illustrates the SA-REST annotations on the text fragment from older Wikipedia page for the subject "computer."

```
(001) <p>
(002) A <b>\textbf{<span class="sem-class" title="http://tap.stanford.edu/#computer">}
      computer \textbf{</span>}</b>
(003) is a <a href="/wiki/Machine" title="Machine">machine</a> that manipulates
(004) <a href="/wiki/Data_(computing)" title="Data (computing)">data</a> according
(005) to a set of <a href="/wiki/Source_code" title="Source code">instructions</a>.
(006) </p>
(007) <p>
(008) \textbf{<span class="domain-rel" title="http://www.owl-ontologies.com/
      ComputingOntology.owl#History_of_Computing">}
(009) Although mechanical examples of computers have existed through much of recorded
      human
(010) history, the first electronic computers were developed in the mid-20th century
      (1940--1945). \textbf{</span>}
</p>
```

Line (002) illustrates the specification of the term *computer* using the *sem-class* property. Lines (008) to (010) exemplify the marking up of the text fragment to indicate that it belongs to the domain *History of Computing*.

SA-REST can also be used to annotate RESTful API descriptions. The following HTML snippet is from the Yahoo! Developer Network mail Web Service API documentation, and the annotation is based on hRESTS [Kopecky et al., 2008].

```
<div class="section domain-rel" lang="en" title="sarest:Service">
  <span class="domain-rel" title="sarest:Operation">
  <div class="titlepage">
    <div>
        <div>    <h3 id="JSON-RPCEndpoint">JSON-RPC Endpoint</h3>
        </div>
    </div>
  </div>
</div>
```

```
<p>The JSON−RPC endpoint implements the <a class ="ulink" href ="http :// json−rpc . org/
    wiki/ specification" target ="top">JSON−RPC spec </a> on top of the Web service .
    Requests are serialized JavaScript following a specific data format .
Each serialized JavaScript object contains the following properties :
</p>

<div class ="itemizedlist domain−rel" title ="sarest :InputMessage">
    <ul >              <li class ="bullist sem−class" title ="sarest :Parameter">
        <code class ="code">method </code >:
            name of the API method being called .
        </li >           ...
    </ul >      </div >
</span >  </div >
```

Here is a simple example of annotating an XHTML block, extracted from the Wikipedia page on hCard, using various annotation formats discussed so far, for comparison.

Plain XHTML

```
<div >     <div >Joe Doe </div >
    <div >604−555−1234 </div >
    <a href ="http :// example .com/" > http :// example .com/ </a>     </div >
```

Annotated with hCard microformat

```
<div class ="vcard">
    <div class ="fn">Joe Doe </div >
    <div class ="tel">604−555−1234 </div >
    <a class ="url" href ="http :// example .com/" > http :// example .com/ </a>
</div >
```

Annotated with Microdata (using schema.org concepts)

```
<div itemscope itemtype ="http :// schema . org/ Person">
    <div itemprop ="name">Joe Doe </div >
    <div itemprop ="telephone">604−555−1234 </div >
    <a itemprop ="url" href =''http :// example .com/" > http :// example .com/ </a>
</div >
```

Annotated with RDFa (using schema.rdfs.org concepts)

```
<div xmlns :schema ="http :// schema . org/"   typeOf ="http :// schema . org/ Person" >
    <div property ="schema :name">Joe Doe </div >
    <div  property ="schema :telephone">604−555−1234 </div >
    <a  rel ="schema :url" href ="http :// example .com/" > http :// example .com/ </a>
</div >
```

Annotated with SA-REST (using schema.org concepts)

```
<div class ="domain−rel" title ="http :// schema . org/ Person" >
    <div class ="sem−class" title ="http :// schema . org/ Person#name">Joe Doe </div >
    <div class ="sem−class" title ="http :// schema . org/ Person#telephone">604−555−1234 </div
        >
    <a class ="sem−rel" title ="http :// schema . org/ Person#url" href =''http :// example .com
        /" > http :// example .com/ </a>
</div >
```

Note that apart from the apparent difference in verbosity, these markups are equivalent. (SA-REST markup can easily be abbreviated by using the familiar namespace rules [to factor `http://schema.org` and `http://scheme.org/Person`], but the current parsers do not support such optimizations yet.)

3.3.6   A STANDARDS-BASED APPROACH TO SPECIFYING EXTRACTION OF RDF TRIPLES

GRDDL is an abbreviation for Gleaning Resource Descriptions from Dialects of Languages [Halpin and Davis, 2007]. It contains markup for declaring that an XML document includes gleanable data (profile) and for linking to algorithms (typically represented in XSLT) for gleaning RDF data from the annotated document (transformation). It can be used in conjunction with RDFa, XHTML, and other XML documents (including with microformats) to obtain RDF triples. See [Connoly, 2007] for detailed examples.

Arenas et al. [2012] describes and illustrates a direct mapping from relational data to RDF model. R2RML is a language for expressing customized mappings from relational databases to RDF datasets [Das et al., 2012]. Such mappings provide the ability to view existing relational data in the RDF data model, expressed in a structure and target vocabulary of the mapping author's choice.

3.3.7   SUMMING IT ALL UP

The Web is morphing from a container of data and documents to hosting the Internet of Things and cyber-physical systems, by connecting and coordinating physical objects with their computational counterparts for sensing and services. In order to realize this future, it is necessary to be able to discover, identify, communicate, and glean functionality of the resources in a standard way. That is, for any Web resource, it is important to determine what it is, what it can do, how we can interact with it, and so on. An enabling technology for doing this can be founded on ontologies, annotations, and standard service interfaces. The following table summarizes the domain, examples of applicable semantic annotation technique, and sample references. The rest of this book will elaborate on the application of these in detail.

Table 3.5: Organization of the rest of the book		
Domain	**Annotation Technique**	**Chapter**
Enterprise Data	RDF/RDFa	4
Services Domain	SA-REST	5
Sensor Data Domain	Model Reference	6
Social Data Domain	Microformat	7
Cloud Computing Data	RDFa	8

CHAPTER 4

Semantics for Enterprise Data

Semantics has played a key role in the evolution of an effective Web infrastructure as well as the next generation of enterprise content management. In both cases, semantics has provided tools to deal with heterogeneity, a massive scale, and the dynamic nature of the content. Ontology is a key component of semantic technologies, which provides the basis for representing, acquiring, and utilizing knowledge. With the availability of several commercial products and many research tools, ontology-driven techniques and systems have already enabled a new generation of industrial strength semantic applications in leading verticals such as financial services, government and intelligence, health-care, pharmaceuticals, and media and entertainment. This chapter focuses on the semantics and enterprise content: it presents the role of semantics in high-end enterprise applications requiring intelligent search, integration and analytics, approaches to create semantic models and annotations, and finally, sample practical applications.

4.1 NATURE OF ENTERPRISE CONTENT AND PROCESSING

The challenges for a modern enterprise information integration system are well understood [Sheth, 1998]. Specifically, the new generation of information integration and analysis software should be able to perform the following tasks:

- Extract, organize, and standardize (or normalize) information from many disparate and heterogeneous content sources (including structured, semi-structured, and unstructured sources) and formats (database tables, XML feeds, PDF files, streaming media, internal documents), and static and dynamic (e.g., database driven) sources that may be internal or external to the organization (including deep Web and open Web).

- For a domain of choice, identify interesting and relevant knowledge (entities like people, places, organizations, and relationships between them) from heterogeneous sources.

- Analyze and correlate extracted information to discover previously unknown or non-obvious relationships between documents and/or entities based on semantics (not syntax) that can help in making business decisions.

- Enable high levels of automation for extraction, normalization, and maintenance of knowledge and content for improved efficiencies of scale.

- Make efficient use of the extracted knowledge and content by providing tools for fast and high-quality (contextual) querying, browsing, and analysis for actionable information.

Practical reality is that an awful lot of enterprise data are locked in Excel spreadsheets and non-database repositories that need to be integrated and analyzed in semantically meaningful ways by providing missing context and surfaced through dashboards and custom portals for business decision making. As noted by Allemang [2010], agility is the key to the success of modern businesses, especially in the face of globalization, the market's appetite for novel products, reliance on complex supply chains and distribution channels, ever-changing international markets and corporate mergers. Information management is at the heart of critical areas such as pharmaceutical research (relying on bioinformatics to clinical trial data), to forecasting in financial sector, to garnering up-to-date military intelligence. In fact, there is a dire need for an *enterprise architecture*, which refers to a description of all the data owned by an enterprise; what role they play in business process, who owns it, how it is managed. Enterprise architecture is particularly important for an agile enterprise, comprising of merged or acquired subsidiaries, new product divisions, and potentially always in flux. Jeff Pollock [Wood, 2010] goes even further: "If information systems are to keep up with businesses, we need to change more than technology—we need to change how people deal with technology."

In the context of eScience, there is a large worldwide infrastructure of computing and data resources that are readily available for scientists to collaborate in virtual laboratories [Atkins, 2003, Hey and Trefethen, 2005]. The rapidly increasing volume of data and high-throughput scientific workflows for analyzing data raise important issues such as:

- How can we leverage the data for critical insights that will in turn drive future research?

- How can we seamlessly manage (compare, integrate, and process) large volumes of data generated by hundreds of distributed laboratories that use heterogeneous materials, equipment, protocols, and parameters?

4.2   ROLE OF SEMANTICS IN THE ENTERPRISE

Decision making requires comparative analysis and aggregation of content from independent sources. In order to manage and use information effectively, three barriers that increase the complexity of managing information have to be overcome: namely, the diverse formats of content, the disparate nature of content, and the need to derive "intelligence" from this content. The key semantic capabilities that can assist here include:

1. *Semantic organization and use of metadata*: Realizing a Semantic Web solution often involves using ontologies [Carrara and Guarino, 1999] to organize domain-specific concepts and relationships, and use of metadata [Klas and Sheth, 1998] to annotate and enrich content.

2. *Semantic normalization*: Normalization done on the basis of semantics plays an important role in dealing with semantic heterogeneity associated with multiple data sources.

3. *Semantic search*: Search effectiveness can be improved by using semantics to overcome the well-known problems of synonymy (co-reference resolution) and polysymy (disambiguation), as well as use relevant background knowledge.

4. *Semantic association*: Semantics can be gleaned by recognizing relevant relationships among concepts [Aleman-meza et al., 2006, Dalvi et al., 2009] and exploited in applications that query data, metadata, and knowledge in an integrated fashion.

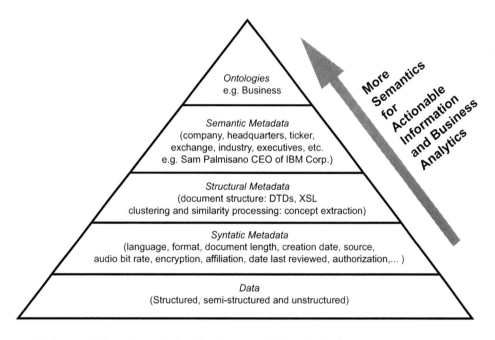

Figure 4.1: Type of Metadata enabling Business Analytics [Sheth, 2003]

Figure 4.1 shows the different types of metadata being employed in an enterprise, and Figure 4.2 shows an annotated document. We discuss below how semantic metadata are created and used within the enterprise.

4.3   CREATION OF SEMANTIC METADATA: MODELS AND ANNOTATIONS

To extract the essence of a document and make it usable, it is necessary to find, analyze, and tag relevant information. The primary impediment to this agenda is the fact that documents usually contain explicit references to specific instances rather than semantic abstractions that are necessary for disambiguation and interpretation. In other words, the necessary parts of semantic metadata (such as categories, classes, column headings, or entities) are normally implicit. So the semantic

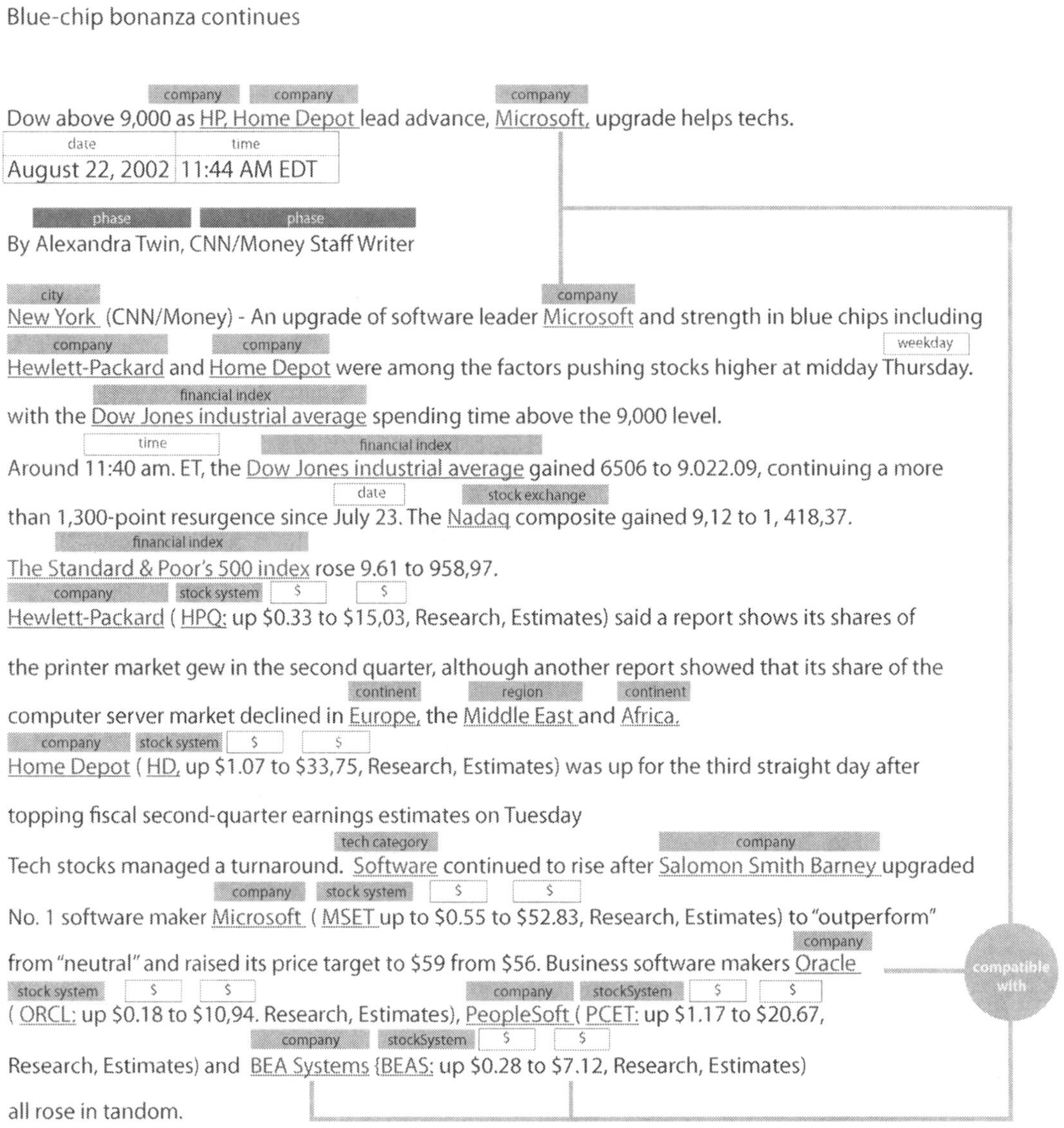
Blue-chip bonanza continues
company
company
company
Dow above 9,000 as HP, Home Depot lead advance, Microsoft, upgrade helps techs.
date
time
August 22, 2002
11:44 AM EDT
phase
phase
By Alexandra Twin, CNN/Money Staff Writer
city
company
New York (CNN/Money) - An upgrade of software leader Microsoft and strength in blue chips including
company
company
weekday
Hewlett-Packard and Home Depot were among the factors pushing stocks higher at midday Thursday.
financial index
with the Dow Jones industrial average spending time above the 9,000 level.
time
financial index
Around 11:40 am. ET, the Dow Jones industrial average gained 6506 to 9.022.09, continuing a more
date
stock exchange
than 1,300-point resurgence since July 23. The Nadaq composite gained 9,12 to 1, 418,37.
financial index
The Standard & Poor's 500 index rose 9.61 to 958,97.
company
stock system
$
$
Hewlett-Packard (HPQ: up $0.33 to $15,03, Research, Estimates) said a report shows its shares of
the printer market gew in the second quarter, although another report showed that its share of the
continent
region
continent
computer server market declined in Europe, the Middle East and Africa.
company
stock system
$
$
Home Depot (HD, up $1.07 to $33,75, Research, Estimates) was up for the third straight day after
topping fiscal second-quarter earnings estimates on Tuesday
tech category
company
Tech stocks managed a turnaround. Software continued to rise after Salomon Smith Barney upgraded
company
stock system
$
$
No. 1 software maker Microsoft (MSET up to $0.55 to $52.83, Research, Estimates) to "outperform"
company
from "neutral" and raised its price target to $59 from $56. Business software makers Oracle
compatible with
stock system
$
$
company
stockSystem
$
$
(ORCL: up $0.18 to $10,94. Research, Estimates), PeopleSoft (PCET: up $1.17 to $20.67,
company
stockSystem
$
$
Research, Estimates) and BEA Systems {BEAS: up $0.28 to $7.12, Research, Estimates)
all rose in tandom.

Figure 4.2: Ontology-based Semantic Metadata Extraction and Enhancement of a Legacy Document [Hammond et al., 2002]

challenge is to infer implicit metadata from instances and available context. Many techniques can be used to extract syntactic and semantic metadata from documents as summarized below:

1. Comprehensive, static, or periodically maintained dictionaries and thesauri can be used to match words and phrases to recognize and normalize domain-specific content terms. Dictionaries such as WordNet can be used to identify and match terms in different directions: finding synonyms or equivalent terms, broader or more general terms, and narrower or more specific terms.

2. Documents can be analyzed for various patterns and co-occurrences using extraction rules to facilitate entity and relationship recognition.

3. Ontologies, capturing domain (application, industry) specific knowledge including entities and relationships, both, at a definitional level (a company has a CEO), and at an instance or assertion level capturing real-world facts or knowledge (Stockholm is the capital of Sweden), can be used. If the ontology deployed is one-size-fits-all and is not domain specific, then the full potential of this approach cannot be exploited (e.g., HP can stand for Hewlett-Packard or Hindustan Petroleum depending on the context).

4. For technical domains, it is also necessary to catalog aliases and acronyms, controlled vocabularies including preferred terms, units of measure equivalency rules, groups of related attribute-value pairs/parameter-settings characterizing processes, etc.

Recall that ontologies consist of definitional aspects like high-level schemas, and assertional aspects like entities, attributes, inter-relationships between entities, domain vocabulary, and factual knowledge—all connected in a semantic manner. As such, ontologies and metadata provide the basis to build tools to organize and provide a useful description of heterogeneous content. In addition to the hierarchical relationship structure of typical taxonomies, ontologies enable cross-node horizontal relationships between entities, thus providing for easy modeling of real-world information requirements. Ontology-driven metadata extraction is *flexible* (assuming the ontology is kept up-to-date to reflect changes in the real world) and *comprehensive* (since it allows modeling of fact-based domain-specific relationships between entities that are at the heart of semantic representations). The entire process requires sophisticated techniques for entity disambiguation and classification to identify the relevant domain or ontology to be used to drive metadata extraction and enhancement. The classifiers can combine probabilistic (Bayesian), learning (Hidden Markov Models), and knowledge-based techniques so that the overall classification accuracy exceeds each classifier's individual accuracy.

To summarize, ontology-driven semantic application development lifecycle (in domains ranging from anti-money laundering and terrorism, to pharmaceutical drug discovery and Glycan structure analysis) has four stages: (1) Creation of a schema that serves as the definitional component of the ontology; (2) Population of the ontology at the instance level; (3) Metadata extraction or semantic annotation of heterogeneous (unstructured, semi-structured, and structured) content from a variety of sources; and (4) Blended Semantic Browsing and Querying (BSBQ) of content to let user seamlessly cross-navigate between related knowledge and content. In other words, a typical ontology-based system provides APIs to query the metadata and knowledge, and builds the application logic and GUI front end for semantic search and/or contextual browsing. Furthermore, to develop active ontologies, there is a need to provide tools to manage requests for new terms, building consensus, resolving provisional terms, and seamlessly integrating frequent updates.

Practical constraints of an enterprise demand relatively smooth transition to new technologies with the ability to bootstrap from legacy data and software. We have already discussed a variety of semantic techniques that capture meaning to different levels of fidelity. As such, it is important to note that a successful application of semantics does not require an overnight transformation of the entire enterprise information space, or force-fitting expressive formal machinery. Instead, it can be approximate and simple at the outset, and evolve over time accruing commensurate benefits.

In order to understand the overall organization of semantic content processing system, consider the architecture of SCORE (Semantic Content Organization and Retrieval Engine) shown in Figure 4.3 [Sheth et al., 2001] (SCORE was subsequently known as Semagix Freedom).

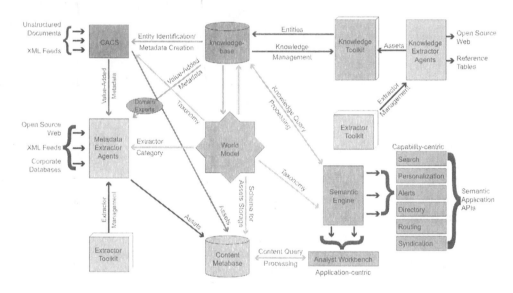

Figure 4.3: SCORE System Architecture [Sheth et al., 2002] (copyright © IEEE, with permission).

Ontologies play a central role in annotating or tagging content. Knowing the context of the content determines which semantic metadata to extract. Automatic classification technology helps select the context. The ontology is divided into two related components—the World Model, which can be seen as the definitional component, and the Knowledgebase, which can be seen as the assertional component. The Knowledgebase reflects that subset of the real world, for which a semantic application is created, and is an important part of the solution. It allows for extraction of value-added semantic metadata and provides the framework for semantic associations. The query processing system provides a reasoning mechanism. A comprehensive suite of APIs support rapid development of semantic applications such as search, directory, personalization, and syndication for small to enterprise-level projects.

The operation of a SCORE technology-based system involves three independent activities as illustrated by the dashed areas in Figure 4.3. They cooperate through XML-based knowledge and metadata sharing.

(i) The first activity (Figure 4.3) involves the definition of the World Model and Knowledgebase. Different parts of the Knowledgebase can be populated from different trusted sources. Various tools help with ambiguity detection and synonym identification. Specifically, classification [Larkey and Croft, 1996, Li and Jain, 1998, Liere and Tadepalli, 1997, Sebastiani, 2002] and Knowledgebase, which exhibit complementary strengths, are employed for resolving ambiguity.

(ii) The second activity (Figure 4.3) is content processing. This includes classification and the extraction of metadata from content. The results are organized according to the World Model definition and stored in the Metabase. Knowledge and content sources can be heterogeneous, internal, or external to the enterprise, and accessible in push (content feeds or database exports) or pull (website) modes.

(iii) The third activity (Figure 4.3) is that of supporting semantic applications. The Semantic Engine processes semantic queries, but does not currently support inference mechanisms found in AI or logic-based systems; instead, it provides limited inference based on the traversal of relationships in the Knowledgebase. An API for building traditional and customized applications is provided with results returned as XML to facilitate GUI creation.

4.3.1   LINKING ENTERPRISE DATA

Current enterprises suffer from having isolated information silos and rapid generation of copious new data. Linking enterprise data [Wood, 2010], using Semantic Web technologies, can help businesses achieve agility. Cross-organizational data integration and sharing should be an ongoing part of data creation and utilization, rather than an afterthought. Furthermore, the linked enterprise data (LED) should try to achieve both machine processing and human comprehension.

A linked data enterprise is an organization in which the act of information creation is intimately coupled with the act of information sharing [Shilovitsky, 2011]. Analogous to the fact that documentation of a system is as important as the construction of the system, in the linked data enterprise, sharing data is as important as producing it. Individuals and groups continue to produce and consume information in ways that are specific to their own business needs, but they produce it in a way that can be connected to other aspects of the enterprise. When the time comes for information to be shared, the investment required to connect it is minimal, and reduces the barriers to information exchange. The motto of information production is "distributed but connectable" [Shilovitsky, 2011].

Ultimately it is important to develop principles, techniques and tools, to author and extract humanreadable and machine-comprehensible parts of a document hand in hand, and keep them side by side [Thirunarayan, 2005].

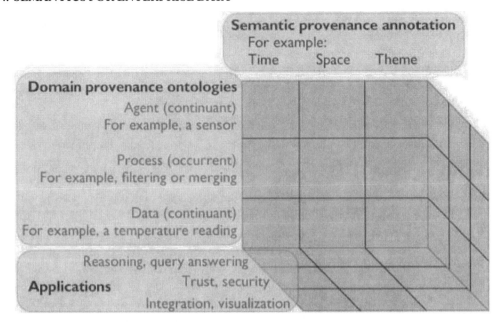

Figure 4.4: The three dimensions of the semantic provenance framework [Sahoo et al., 2008]

4.3.2   SEMANTIC METADATA IN ESCIENCE

Semantic metadata is being harvested and used in a broad range of applications spanning from search engines to data analytics to biomedical and health informatics. As a case study, we discuss our research and development efforts on the use of semantic metadata in eScience.

In eScience, provenance information metadata are especially critical for effective management of increasing volumes of scientific data from industrial-scale experiment protocols. The semantic provenance framework for eScience data comprises expressive provenance information and domain-specific provenance ontologies that let software applications unambiguously and reliably interpret data in the correct context [Sahoo, 2010]. Specific motivating factors for using semantic metadata are

- to create a conceptual context and for accurate data interpretation,

- to use as a basis for data quality and trust, and

- to support interoperability and integration using ontology mapping and merging of semantic metadata that subscribe to different ontologies.

For example, PROV Ontology (PROV-O[1]) expresses the PROV Data Model using the OWL2 Web Ontology Language (OWL2) by providing a set of classes, properties, and restrictions

---

[1]http://www.w3.org/TR/prov-o/

that can be used to represent and interchange provenance information generated in different systems and under different contexts. It can also be specialized to create new classes and properties to model provenance information for different applications and domains. Provenance metadata records the *how, where, what, when, why, which,* and by *whom* of data generated in a scientific experiment [Goble, 2002, Simmhan et al., 2005, Stevens et al., 2007, Tan, 2007]. As such, it lets researchers verify and validate experimental procedures. *Semantic provenance* is information created with reference to a formal knowledge model or an ontology that imposes a domain-specific provenance view on scientific data. It consists of formally defined concepts linked together using named relationships with a set of rules to represent domain constraints. Semantic provenance is more general than system provenance. We illustrate the distinction between system provenance and semantic provenance using two types of queries. Consider the query: "Find the original data from which result datum X was derived." This type of query is answered using system provenance. It uses the workflow-centric provenance information that documents the invocation order of processes, the input data, and the output data for each process. So, using the links connecting a process's output data to its input data, a provenance-aware system could trace and identify the original data entity for result data X. Scientists typically use queries in this category to investigate the protocol that generated the data and to rerun a scientific workflow if needed for validation. In contrast, consider the query from the proteomics domain: "Find proteins composed of peptides with N-glycosylation consensus sequence {*N[^P][S/T]*} identified in samples labeled with O18." This type of query is answered using semantic provenance. Queries in this category are complex and involve relationships that tie data, processes, and equipment parameters together using a domain-specific conceptual view.

4.3.3   SEMANTIC TECHNIQUES IN ESCIENCE

We now describe the semantic issues for eScience.

The semantic provenance framework for eScience can be analyzed along three fundamental dimensions (see Figure 4.4):

- semantic provenance annotation,

- domain provenance ontologies, and

- usage.

The first dimension involves a set of specialized tools plugged into a scientific workflow on demand to create semantic-provenance information. Extracting comprehensive metadata from multiple sources, such as generated scientific data and Web forms (for parameter specifications, equipment details, project details, and so forth) is another important element of this dimension. The second dimension uses domain-specific provenance ontologies to model scientific processes, data (including temporal information), and agents as formally defined concepts linked together using named relationships. In the third dimension, software agents use reasoning tools to process the semantic-provenance information and answer complex domain queries. They can also use semantic-provenance information to compare, integrate, retrieve, and visualize scientific data. In summary, semantic provenance addresses four requirements: (i) provenance information interoperability, (ii) ease of application development, (iii) precise description of provenance, and (iv) inferencing capability and digital representation of provenance. Semantic provenance also addresses three nonfunctional requirements: (i) use of publicly available ontologies, (ii) support for storage and querying of resources, and (iii) development of visualization tools for Semantic Web resources.

4.4   EXAMPLES OF SEMANTIC ENTERPRISE APPLICATIONS

There are a number of ways to classify applications built using ontologies and the Semantic (Web) technologies. We use a simple classification that is a function of the complexity and the depth of semantics:

- **Semantic search and contextual browsing**:
  Semantic search engines use ontologies consisting of general interest areas (such as news, sports, business, and entertainment), and provide domain specific search (search based on relevant, domain specific attributes) and contextual browsing of textual and multi-media content from hundreds of sources.

- **Semantic integration**:
  In equity analytics application [Sheth et al., 2002], textual and audio-video content can be aggregated from various websites and NewsML feeds originating from hundreds of local and international sources, and continuously classified using a small taxonomy, for automatically extracting domain-specific metadata (after a one-time effort to semi-automatically create a source-specific extractor agent). The equity market ontology used by such an application consists of millions of facts including entity and relationship instances. An illustrative example of a complex semantic query involving metadata and ontology is: Show analyst reports (from many sources in various formats) that are competitors of Intel Corporation. In Repertoire Management application for multinational entertainment conglomerate, the ontology contains tens of millions of instances (of semantically disambiguated names of artists, track names, etc), and heterogeneity can be overcome by providing uniform and integrated access to content in the company's extensive media database.

- **Analytics and Knowledge Discovery**:
  In Passenger Threat Assessment application for national/homeland security and Anti-money laundering application, the ontology is populated from many public, licensed, and proprietary knowledge sources, and is kept up-to-date with changes in knowledge sources on a daily basis. The resulting ontology has over a million instances. Furthermore, metadata are extracted periodically or continuously from tens of heterogeneous sources (150 file formats, HTML, XML feeds, dynamic websites, relational databases, etc.) [Dill et al., 2003, Hammond et al., 2002] in a scalable manner using current computing technology. Another example of enterprise data analytics and integration involves information extraction from legacy heterogeneous

materials and process specification documents (specs) critical to aerospace and automotive industries [Thirunarayan, 2005]. Specs present numeric data with accompanying text and graphics that explain the quantitative information, and are used extensively by sales personnel, design engineers, manufacturing engineers, and quality assurance personnel. *In order to do any meaningful analysis, comparison, and integration of specs, one should first extract numerical, tabular, or graphical data and operate on that data in the fashion intended by its meaning.* (For instance, does a given numeric value with a unit of measure represent a process parameter or a material property, which are very different in nature? Is it maximum or typical or minimum value? Is percentage specification by weight or by volume? Has the table value been modified by a footnote?) According to Thirunarayan et al. [2005], computer-assisted content extraction involves two steps: (a) recognize structure and domain library concepts (terms, attribute-value pairs, and procedures [grouped/related pairs]) present in a spec, and (b) reorganize it to generate its formalization. *A semi-automatic approach to extraction improves both the quality and the efficiency of extraction to the extent that mechanical and routine aspects of extraction can be codified and automated, while simultaneously deferring the more difficult and irregular portions to a human.*

Google Refine is a power tool for working with messy data, cleaning it up by removing inconsistencies and redundancies, transforming it from one format into another, extending it with Web services, and linking it to databases [Huynh and Mazzocchi, 2011]. Refine can be used to integrate independent data silos, eventually assisting in mapping data into RDF data stores for analysis.[2] This tool has already impacted open government data and journalism communities.

We also summarize the application of semantic provenance framework in the glycoproteomics domain. Mass spectrometry (MS) is an analytical procedure for proteomics data to study protein structures and post-translational modifications. Software tools analyze raw data produced by a mass spectrometer in a multistep process that yields a list of identified entities and their quantification. Scientists originally conducted this analytical procedure manually by transferring data across distributed systems and then invoking software tools. The scientists, who were responsible for keeping track of each result file across multiple projects, often spent frustratingly long hours searching for a previous result or trying to correlate results using handwritten notes. This analytical process can be completely automated as a scientific workflow using Semantic Web services (Web services annotated with ontological concepts) orchestrated using the Taverna[3] workflow engine. To help scientists manage the large volumes of data using provenance information, the ProPreO proteomics[4] provenance ontology was developed. The service infrastructure implements a set of semantic-provenance creation services that can be used to create semantic provenance in two phases. The first phase is entity extraction that are categorized as instances of ProPreO ontology classes using class membership relations based on a set of heuristic rules. The entity extraction and classification at each step of the workflow results in an aggregated list of ProPreO ontology class instances at the end of the

---

[2]http://logd.tw.rpi.edu/technology/rdf_extension_google_refine
[3]http://www.taverna.org.uk/
[4]http://lsdis.cs.uga.edu/projects/glycomics/propreo/

workflow. During the second phase, the provenance-creation services assert named relationships that apply between two entities (categorized as instances of ProPreO classes in the previous step), using the ProPreO ontology schema as reference. The implementation uses tools such as Jena, Oracle 10g database, and SPARQL query interface to query the semantic provenance. As a sample query, consider the following:

> *List the protein groups identified with high confidence value—that is, protein groups with a Mascot score > 3500—detected by the Mascot search engine against a T.cruzi database (Mascot search input parameter, Taxonomy = T.cruzi). The protein groups should contain at least one peptide fragment with a specific consensus sequence of* {*N[^P][S/T]*}.

This query seeks to identify the best-quality results from all the sample runs executed until the current date to identify and integrate data from multiple result files. This framework can also be applied to model provenance information of sensor data related to weather forecasting. The ProPreO ontology can be extended to incorporate a Nuclear Magnetic Resonance (NMR)-based data-analysis protocol. This will let software applications use semantic provenance information to create an unambiguous context for comparing experimental data for toxicology metabolomics using MS-based and NMR-based data-analysis approaches.

To better situate the current methodology and to shed light on practical issues relevant to building the real world applications, we review some empirical observations. Ontology captures shared knowledge by representing a part of the domain or the real world around which the semantic application revolves. It is the "ontological commitment" reflecting agreement among the experts defining the ontology and its uses that is the basis for the "semantic normalization" necessary for semantic integration. Our observations break down as follows:

- **Ontology Depth, Expressiveness**

    - Many real-world ontologies may be described as semi-formal ontologies (as opposed to formal ontologies) that may be populated with partial or incomplete knowledge, may contain occasional inconsistencies, or occasionally violate constraints (e.g., all schema-level constraints may not be observed in the knowledge base that instantiates the ontology schema). Such situations are unavoidable when the ontology is populated by many persons or by extracting and integrating knowledge from multiple sources [Gruber, 2003].

    - Formal or semi-formal ontologies represented in very expressive languages (compared to moderately expressive ones) have, in practice, yielded little value in some real-world applications. Practical applications often end up using languages that lie closer to less expressive languages in the "expressiveness vs. computational complexity continuum." For example, in a financial industry domain, it is important to develop precise term definitions and synonyms for use by diverse stakeholders such as brokers, traders, and the exchange, and design tools that provide data/ontology views akin to spreadsheets and block diagrams for use by domain experts. On the other hand, we have also seen applications, especially in scientific domains such as biology, where more expressive languages are needed, and even OWL is inadequate.

- As we go from less demanding search/browsing/personalization to more demanding integration/portal applications to even more demanding analytical/business intelligence/knowledge discovery applications, there is a greater need for deeper (domain- and task-specific) semantic metadata. Also needed is a processing and application logic shift from entities/concepts to relationships. Query processing requirements also become increasingly demanding for analytical applications.

- **Ontology Scope**

  - Currently, enterprise applications have an ontological commitment that is only enterprise-wide, even though the data/content involved in the application may involve a combination of proprietary data within enterprise, subscribed/syndicated content, and open source (Web) content. For example, industry-sector-analyst classification and instance data can vary between two brokerage houses. While broad industry wide ontologies and knowledge bases typically involve strong social processes involving years of committee efforts, typical ontologies for Enterprise applications are narrow, domain, or task/application ontologies (e.g., initial effort may focus on ontology for anti-money laundering, rather than entire financial services domain) that require strong tools that IT professionals and domain experts can use to design the ontology schema and populate the ontology from a few high quality knowledge sources. Sometimes ontologies may be bootstrapped using existing database schemas and industry-wide metadata standards but involve substantial modeling efforts.

- **Ontology Size and Knowledge/Metadata Extraction**

  - Ontology population is critical. Furthermore, it is necessary to keep these ontologies up-to-date with facts and knowledge on a timely basis ("active ontologies"). Both the scale and freshness requirements dictate that populating ontologies with instance data need to be automated.

  - Large-scale metadata extraction and semantic annotation are possible. However, the general trade off of depth versus scale applies.

- **Semantic Operations**

  - A vast majority of the Semantic (Web) applications that have been developed or envisioned rely on three crucial capabilities: ontology creation, semantic annotation, and querying/inferencing. All these capabilities must scale to many millions of documents and concepts (rather than hundreds to thousands) for current applications. In fact, applications requiring billions of documents and concepts have also been explored.

  - Two of the most fundamental problems for which semantic techniques have been developed are: named entity identification/recognition[5] and semantic ambiguity[6] resolution.

[5]http://en.wikipedia.org/wiki/Named-entity_recognition
[6]http://en.wikipedia.org/wiki/Polysemy

Named entity recognition (NER) is the process of finding and classifying mentions of persons, organizations, locations, etc., in text. Semantic ambiguity arises when a word or phrase has widely differing meanings. Typically, contextual information is employed to resolve the ambiguity. Without good solutions to these problems, none of the applications listed will be of any practical use. Solving both these problems require highly multidisciplinary approaches, borrowing from NLP/lexical analysis, statistical and IR techniques, and possibly machine learning techniques. A high degree of automation is possible in meeting many real-world semantic disambiguation requirements, although pathological cases will always exist and complete automation is unlikely.

– Support for heterogeneous content is key—it is too hard to deploy separate products within a single enterprise to deal with structured, semi-structured, and unstructured data/content management. New applications involve extensive types of heterogeneity in format, media and access/delivery mechanisms (e.g., a news feed in RSS, NewsML news, a Web posted article in HTML or served up dynamically through a database query and XSLT transformation, analyst report in PDF or WORD, subscription service with API-based access to Lexis/Nexis, enterprise's own relational databases and content management systems, e-mails). Database researchers have long studied the issue of integrating heterogeneous data, and many of the techniques to deal with semantic heterogeneity come in handy, especially at the schema levels, but a broader array of techniques are required (including statistical, lexical/NLP, and machine learning) to deal with instance level heterogeneity. And while the enterprise no longer wishes to be divided between separate worlds of structured and unstructured data management, the middle ground of semi-structured data (XML-based data and RDF-based metadata) is growing at an explosive rate.

– Semantic query processing with the ability to query both ontology and metadata to retrieve heterogeneous content is highly valuable. Furthermore, high performance and highly scalable query processing techniques that deal with more complex representations compared to database schemas and with more explicit roles of relationships are important. Database techniques are already being adapted to deal with large RDF/triple stores.

Industries or areas where early applications used semantic technologies include [Cardoso et al., 2007, Sheth and Stephens, 2007] health care and life sciences [Baker and Cheung, 2007, Sheth, 2006, Sheth et al., 2006a], financial services [Lara et al., 2007, Sheth, 2005, Sheth et al., 2002], national security and intelligence [Avant et al., 2002, Golbeck et al., 2006, Sheth et al., 2005a], and pharmaceutical and drug development [Goble et al., 2005, Neumann, 2005, Neumann and Quan, 2006].

CHAPTER 5

Semantics for Services

A Web service is an application that provides a Web API that enables communication using XML and the Web. Service-Oriented Architecture (SOA) describes a set of common design practices for service-based applications. It defines mechanisms for describing services, advertising and discovering services, and communicating with services. SOA is based on the request/response paradigm where an application is modularized and presented as services for client applications. Application developers and system integrators can build applications by composing one or more services without knowing their implementation details. While the current focus is on using the standards-based services to establish static connections between various components, businesses are also exploring issues such as reuse, interoperability, and agility. Realizing the potential benefits of SOA requires semi-automated and automated techniques and tools for searching or locating services, selecting suitable ones, composing them into complex processes, resolving heterogeneity issues through process and data mediation, reducing manual effort. In this chapter, we discuss how semantics can be leveraged for searching and composing services, and how it can help achieve a greater level of automation to service orientation.

5.1 NATURE OF WEB SERVICES

SOA has been offered as a panacea for enterprise application integration, implementation of inter-organizational business processes, and for the development of all complex distributed applications. SOA promises greater reuse of services, ease of interoperability between SOA services, and greater agility in the business processes. However, achieving any of these places a greater burden on the specification of the services and processes. One of the fundamental building blocks of SOA-based solutions is creating self-describing services that can be reused across various applications. *It is not enough to know the interface that a service presents; it is critical to know exactly what functionality a service provides or what behavior a service exhibits.* Note that an interface tells us how to invoke a service; it is the functional specification that tells us what the service does.

The Web Service Description Language (WSDL[1]) has been created specifically for the purpose of describing Web services. It provides several useful constructs for describing services, including:

- Operation constructs to describe service methods, provide information about parameters, and define types of operations (synchronous, asynchronous);

[1]http://en.wikipedia.org/wiki/Web_Services_Description_Language

- Operation parameter descriptions via the XML schema; and

- Information about the type of protocol needed to invoke the service.

Simple Object Access Protocol (SOAP[2]) over HTTP, is a protocol specification for exchanging structured information in the implementation of Web Services in computer networks. Universal Description, Discovery, and Integration (UDDI)[3] is a directory service where Web services can be registered and searched.

REpresentational State Transfer (REST) (as proposed by Fielding [2000]) is an architecture style for designing networked applications that provides a lightweight alternative to Remote Procedure Call (RPC) mechanisms such as, Java-RMI (Remote Method Invocation), CORBA (Common Object Request Broker Architecture), and Web Services (SOAP, WSDL). According to Fielding [2000]: "Representational state transfer is intended to evoke an image of how a well-designed Web application behaves: a network of web pages (a virtual state-machine), where the user progresses through an application by selecting links (state transitions), resulting in the next page containing links (representing the next state of the application and its transitions) being transferred to the user and rendered for their use." RESTful applications use HTTP to connect with and communicate between machines, and for implementing all four CRUD (Create/Read/Update/Delete) operations. Zuzak [2010] provides a good introduction to REST and Zuzak et al. [2011] gives a formalization of RESTful services using finite-state machines. To illustrate REST-philosophy, consider the example of querying a phonebook application for user details. Given a UserID, using Web Services and SOAP, the request sent (using an HTTP POST request) to the server looks something like this:

```
<?xml version="1.0" encoding="UTF8"?>
  <soap:Envelope xmlns:soap="http://www.w3.org/2001/12/soap-envelope" soap:
     encodingStyle="http://www.w3.org/2001/12/soap-encoding">
    <soap:body pb="http://www.acme.com/phonebook">
       <pb:GetUserDetails>
            <pb:UserID>70007</pb:UserID>
       </pb:GetUserDetails>
    </soap:Body>
  </soap:Envelope>
```

The response is an XML file with embedded payload inside a SOAP response envelope.

With REST, the client references the Web resource using a URL (one URL for each UserID) sent to the server using a simpler GET request: `http://www.acme.com/phonebook/UserDetails/70007`. The response is an XML file with user details.

Web Services often require libraries to create the SOAP/HTTP request and parse the SOAP response, while, with REST, a simple HTTP network connection is enough. The REST approach creates a resource for every service, and identifies each resource using a logical (not physical) URL. The logical URL is mapped to a static physical URL or to a dynamically generated file, as the service deems fit [Costello and Kehoe, 2005]. REST can easily handle more complex requests (such

---

[2]`http://en.wikipedia.org/wiki/SOAP`
[3]`http://en.wikipedia.org/wiki/Universal_Description_Discovery_and_Integration`

as involving full name) using multiple parameters (composed using a form) as shown: `http://www.acme.com/phonebook/UserDetails?firstName=James&lastName=Bond`. If the parameters are long or in binary form, HTTP POST requests are used, and include the parameters in the POST body. As a rule, GET requests should be for read-only queries, and POST requests should be used for creating, updating, and deleting data. By using XML-based messaging, RESTful services can bring together discrete data from different services to create meaningful mashups [Worthen, 2007]. Several companies are developing tools to enable the creation of mashups with little or no programming knowledge. Unfortunately, these tools are limited in the number of services with which they can interact—typically, they deal with services internal to the company that created them or to services that have standard types of outputs such as RSS or Atom. This limits the scalability of service composition. Thus, independent of the technologies used, the development of service-oriented applications remains limited, falling short of the promised simplicity for constructing agile and interoperable systems. The fundamental reason for this is the practical difficulties in discovering sets of suitable services, interpreting them, developing software that overcomes their inherent data and process mismatches, and finally combining them into a complex composite process.

For completeness, we recapitulate terminology used in the Semantic Web services (SWS) field to identify the main tasks and concepts [Pedrinaci et al., 2011]: *Crawling* is the task of locating all available services on the Web, typically available in the form of WSDL files or HTML pages describing Web APIs. *Discovery* involves searching for services that are able to fulfill certain user requirements. In general, it subsumes both service crawling and service matching. *Matching, or matchmaking*, is the task of identifying Web service advertisements that satisfy the requested Web service function. *Ranking* is the task of ordering matched Web services according to a set of preferences specified in terms of the non-functional properties of Web services. *Selection* is the task of selecting one service to use from a (ranked) list of viable Web services. This is usually done manually. *Composition* is the task of combining Web services in order to achieve a complex task. The result of composition is an orchestration of Web services, via a plan. *Orchestration* defines the sequence and conditions for the enactment of Web services in order to achieve a complex objective by appropriately combining the functionality provided by existing Web services. Orchestration defines the data-flow (i.e., how the data are propagated and used throughout the process) and the control-flow (i.e., when should a certain activity be executed). *Choreography* describes the interactions of services with their users (man or machine). It defines the expected behavior of a Web service, that is, the exchanged messages, from a client's point of view. Choreography interpretation leads to a successful invocation of a Web service independently of how the execution of the Web service is performed internally. *Mediation* is necessary in environments with heterogeneous components. Mediation is a principle by which an intermediate element, a mediator, is introduced between two elements to resolve their heterogeneities without having to adapt one or the other. Issues concerning terminology and data representation are commonly referred to as data mediation, and handled using ontology mapping/transformation. Protocol mediation aims at achieving a successful interaction between two processes (or Web services) by ensuring that message exchanges between the processes are harmonious. *Invocation* is concerned with the actual call to an operation of a Web service. Invocation is therefore closely related to choreographies in that the latter will specify an order for performing a set of invocations. *Grounding* specifies how certain activities are mapped into low-level operations with Web services. *Lifting* refers to the transformation of information from its representation at the syntactic level used by the Web service (typically XML) into its semantic counterpart (such as, RDF, OWL, WSML). *Lowering* refers to the transformation of information represented in a semantic formalism into some syntactic encoding that can be used for communicating with the Web service. Lowering and lifting are inverses of each other, and are often described in EXtensible Stylesheet Language (XSLT [4]).

5.2   ROLE OF SEMANTICS IN WEB SERVICES

A service is a provider-client interaction that creates and captures the value. The Semantic Services Science (3S) model uses ontology-based semantic modeling and descriptions to capture technical, human, organizational, and business value aspects. Figure 5.1 shows various components of a service and their relationship. The central entity is the organization that consumes or offers services. A service is realized using the assets that the organization possesses. The assets include software, hardware, intellectual property, and human assets. Software assets include any software, applications, or infrastructural components that can be converted to services or used to create services. From an implementation point of view, the software assets may convert to services by either using Web service technologies (WSDL, SOAP, UDDI) or lightweight approaches like REST and AJAX. Human assets include project managers, software developers, customer relationship representatives and other relevant persons involved with creating, developing, marketing, maintaining, or otherwise managing the service.

To understand and use a service, a client must understand the semantics of each service operation. In other words, the client must be able to unambiguously decipher each operation's intended purpose as well as the intended content of all elements of its parameters. The service providers and clients have three potential options for addressing this issue:

- Pre-agreement on all terms for operation names and parameters between service providers and clients. This approach requires a manual agreement between the service provider and potential clients before they can access the service.

- Documentation of all aspects of a service. This approach lets clients read documentation to understand how to use a particular service. Interoperability is based on how well application developers understand textual descriptions (documenting behavior informally).

- Service elements annotated with terms from domain models including industry standards, vocabularies, taxonomies, and ontologies. This approach overcomes the need to create agreements with all potential clients, and alleviates or eliminates terminological discrepancy. Moreover, if

[4] http://www.w3.org/TR/xslt20/

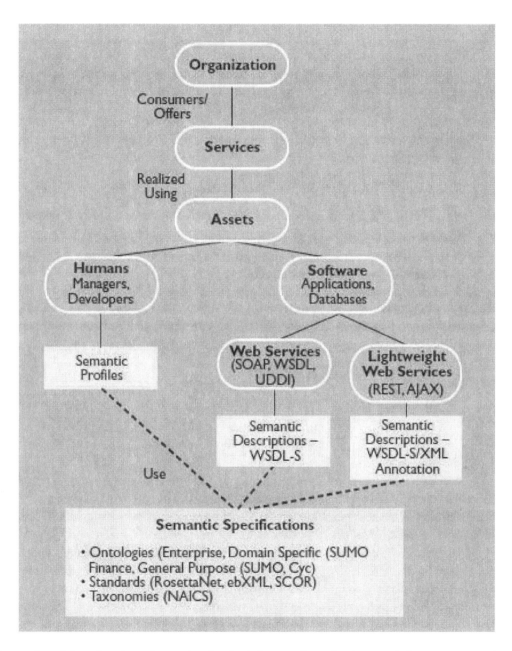

Figure 5.1: A broader view of a service that includes people, technology, and the organizational perspective [Sheth et al., 2006b] (copyright © ACM, with permission).

the service provider uses a formal modeling language for annotating the services, machines can process the annotations and ease the human effort required to determine the service's use.

SWS were proposed whereby intelligent agents would be able to exploit semantic descriptions in order to carry out complex tasks on behalf of humans. The early works on SWS combined semantic Web, Agents, and Web services technologies. To address the challenges of specifying SWS, four types of semantics were proposed and first used in the METEOR-S project (see Figure 5.2):

- *Functional Semantics*—A formal description of the service's functionality, for efficient discovery and reuse [Verma et al., 2005].

- *Data Semantics*—A formal description of the data the services exchange, for achieving inter-operability [Nagarajan et al., 2006].

- *Non-functional Semantics*—A formal description of the service-level agreements and quality of service attributes, for service providers to differentiate themselves from their competitors [Cardoso et al., 2004, Oldham, 2006].

- *Execution Semantics*—A formal model of the Web service's runtime behavior and exceptions, for ensuring that services execute correctly and for supporting run-time exceptions [Verma, 2006].

The essential characteristic of SWS is therefore the use of languages with well-defined semantics covering the subset of the above mentioned categories that are amenable to automated reasoning. Several languages have been used so far including those from the Semantic Web, e.g., RDF(S) and OWL, SWS-specific languages such as the Web Service Modeling Language (WSML), and others originating from research on Knowledge-Based Systems such as F-Logic and OCML. See Figure 5.3 for a brief comparative analysis of four SWS formalisms.

A critical problem for enterprises is finding services that they can reuse across entire business processes. A functional description of the service "along with a discovery mechanism that can leverage the description" is the key to increasing reuse in enterprises. An immediate impact of data semantics specification is the better support for data mediation and service interoperability.

In the context of composing RESTful services, the problems with interoperability and integration can be traced to dealing with data through purely syntactic and structural means. Instead, semantic techniques are required. If a company developing a mashup tool wanted to add a new service that did not have a standard output or that was not internal to the tool, it could modify its existing tooling in order to incorporate the new service's interface. However, this solution is neither modular nor scalable because of the rate at which new services are coming online. As discussed later, semantic annotation of RESTful services can be harnessed for data mediation and service composition in mashups, to improve modularity and scalability.

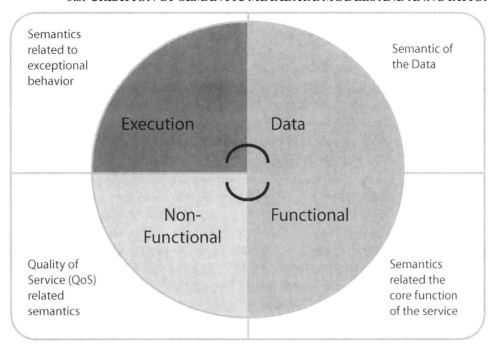

Figure 5.2: The Four Types of Semantics [Pedrinaci et al., 2011, Sheth, 2003]

Specification	Description	Formalism
OWL-S	An OWL-based upper ontology semantically representing Web services.	Description logics
SWSL (Semantic Web Service Language)	A combination first order logic and rules to represent Web services.	First order logic, Different variants of rule languages (Horn, Hilog, and so forth)
WSDL-S, SAWSDL	Use of extensibility elements in WSDL to annotate elements with terms in ontologies.	Agnostic (examples typically use description logics, but use of UML for conceptual modeling is also recognized)
WSMO	A F-logic based conceptual model for representing Web services.	F-logic

Figure 5.3: A comparison of four Semantic Web service specifications

5.3 CREATION OF SEMANTIC METADATA: MODELS AND ANNOTATIONS

There are two broad approaches to specifying SWS. One alternative represents a revolutionary rethinking of all aspects of semantic services (exemplified by OWL-S[5] and WSMO,[6] while the

[5]http://www.daml.org/services/owl-s/

other alternative represents an evolutionary approach that is compatible with the existing standards and industrial practices. The latter is accomplished using WSDL's extensibility elements to provide hooks for semantically annotating various service elements [Huynh and Mazzocchi, 2011, Sivashanmugam et al., 2003]. This research has culminated in Semantic Annotation of Web Services (SAWSDL) [Kopecky et al., 2007, Sheth et al., 2008a] becoming a W3C candidate recommendation in early 2007 [Akkiraju et al., 2005]. SAWSDL[7] defines a set of extension attributes for the WSDL (and XML Schema definition language) that allows description of additional semantics of WSDL components. The specification defines how semantic annotation is accomplished using references to semantic models, e.g., ontologies. SAWSDL does not specify a language for representing the semantic models. Instead it provides mechanisms by which concepts from the semantic models, typically defined outside the WSDL document, can be referenced from within WSDL components using annotations.

For an open, flexible, and standards-based approach to adding semantics to RESTful services, SA-REST grounds service descriptions to semantic metamodels via model reference annotations, similarly to SAWSDL. Specifically, SA-REST[8] is a microformat to add additional metadata to (but not limited to) REST API descriptions in HTML and XHTML [Sheth et al., 2007]. Developers can directly embed metadata from various models such an ontology, taxonomy, or a tag cloud into their API descriptions. The embedded metadata can be used to improve search (e.g., perform faceted search for APIs), data mediation (in conjunction with XML annotation), as well as help in easier integration of services to create mashups.

5.3.1   TOP-DOWN APPROACH EXEMPLIFIED

OWL-S is based on the definition of high-level ontologies providing expressive frameworks for describing Web services.

Benefits of OWL-S

OWL-S [Martin et al., 2004] is an upper-level ontology[9] in OWL for describing SWS. OWL-S defines an ontology along three main aspects:

- The *Service Profile* describes "what the service does" in terms of inputs, outputs, preconditions, and effects (IOPEs);

- The *Service Model* describes "how a service works" in terms of a process model that may describe a complex behavior over underlying services; and

- The *Service Grounding* describes "how the service can be accessed," usually by grounding to WSDL.

[6]http://www.wsmo.org
[7]http://www.w3.org/2001/sw/wiki/SAWSDL
[8]http://www.w3.org/Submission/SA-REST/
[9]An upper-level ontology (aka top-level ontology or foundation ontology) describes very general concepts that are the same across all knowledge domains.

The Service Profile provides the core functional description of services and is used for advertising. This description is suitable for software agents to discover relevant services. The Service Model informs clients about service usage by specifying the semantic content of requests, replies, and pre-conditions, and how clients have to invoke the service. Reasoning support for OWL-S is provided primarily by OWL-DL reasoner, which has its limitations for defining preconditions and effects. OWL-S distinguishes three kinds of processes: atomic processes, composite processes, and simple processes. *Atomic processes* are processes that are directly invocable. *Composite processes* are processes that require several steps in the interaction and/or multi server actions. In order to support the definition of composite processes, OWL-S provides a set of block-oriented control constructs, such as Sequence, If-Then-Else, or Repeat While. *Simple processes* provide an abstraction mechanism able to provide multiple views over existing atomic and composite processes. Simple processes are not directly invocable (they are not associated with a grounding), although they have single-step interactions much like atomic processes. The Service Grounding provides the details necessary for invoking the service. It is therefore concerned with aspects such as the protocol to be used, the message format, their serialization, the transport protocol, and the address of the endpoint to be invoked. OWL-S does not predefine the language to be used for grounding; however, due to its wide adoption, a reference grounding implementation is provided for WSDL.

The following listing shows an example of an atomic process [van Der Aalst et al., 2003].

```
<process:AtomicProcess rdf:ID="Purchase">
  <process:hasInput>
    <process:Input rdf:ID="ObjectPurchased"/>
  </process:hasInput>
  <process:hasInput>
    <process:Input rdf:ID="PurchaseAmt"/>
  </process:hasInput>
  <process:hasInput>
    <process:Input rdf:ID="CreditCard"/>
  </process:hasInput>
  <process:hasOutput>
    <process:Output rdf:ID="ConfirmationNum"/>
    </process:hasOutput>
  <process:hasResult>
    <process:Result>
        <process:hasResultVar>
          <process:ResultVar rdf:ID="CreditLimH">
              <process:parameterType rdf:resource="&ecom;#Dollars"/>
          </process:ResultVar>
          </process:hasResultVar>
        <process:inCondition>
        <expr:KIF-Condition>
            <expr:expressionBody>
              (and (current-value (credit-limit ?CreditCard)
                                  ?CreditLimH)
                    (>= ?CreditLimH ?purchaseAmt))
            </expr:expressionBody>
        </expr:KIF-Condition>
        </process:inCondition>
          <process:withOutput>
```

```
< process : OutputBinding >
    < process : toParam   rdf : resource ="#ConfirmationNum"/ >
    < process : valueFunction   rdf : parseType ="Literal">
        <cc : ConfirmationNum   xsd : datatype ="&xsd ;# string "/ >
    </ process : valueFunction >
</ process : OutputBinding >
    </ process : withOutput >
    < process : hasEffect >
        < expr : KIF—Condition >
            < expr : expressionBody >
                (and  (confirmed  (purchase  ?purchaseAmt)  ?ConfirmationNum)
                    (own  ?objectPurchased)
                    (decrease  (credit —limit  ?CreditCard)
                        ?purchaseAmt))
            </ expr : expressionBody >
        </ expr : KIF—Condition >
    </ process : hasEffect >
    </ process : Result >
</ process : hasResult >
</ process : AtomicProcess >
```

5.3.2   BOTTOM-UP APPROACH EXEMPLIFIED

WSDL-S [Akkiraju et al., 2005] is a light-weight approach to associating semantics with Web Services that served as a precursor to SAWSDL and SA-REST. Figure 5.4 shows various types of heterogeneity and how SWS can bridge it. Figure 5.5 shows examples of heterogeneities and specific methods to overcome them. The basic annotations that SAWSDL or SA-REST adds are inputs, outputs, operations, interfaces, and faults. The annotation of a concept in SAWSDL or SA-REST ties that concept to an ontology or a conceptual model. Neither SAWSDL nor SA-REST enforce the choice of language for representing ontology, but allow use of OWL or RDF. SAWSDL annotations are added to formal service descriptions in WSDL (in the form of bits of XML representing URIs of ontology objects embedded as properties in WSDL), while SA-REST annotations are added to textual service descriptions in XHTML pages. Thus, adding semantics to REST is more challenging than adding semantics to WSDL because it adds semantic annotations only to those page elements that wrap a service or a service description. Consequently, SA-REST uses RDFa[10] and Gleaning Resource Descriptions from Dialects of Languages (GRDDL[11]) to add and capture annotations.

Canonical data models are excellent for supporting interoperability within and among enterprises. Because many applications already have their own schema, application developers often create mappings between application specific schema and canonical data models for interoperability. In SAWSDL, the *modelReference* and *schemaMapping* attributes are the most appropriate for this task (see Figure 5.6). The schemaMapping annotation is decomposed into two different extension attributes, namely *liftingSchemaMapping* and *loweringSchemaMapping*, so as to specifically identify the type of transformation performed. Fortunately, SAWSDL is agnostic to both the domain model and the mapping language, which gives it flexibility: domain models can be as simple as agreed

[10]http://www.w3.org/TR/xhtml-rdfa-primer/
[11]http://www.w3.org/TR/grddl/

Type of Heterogeneities	Approaches to Resolve Heterogeneities
Interaction Protocol/Execution Level Difference in interaction protocol of services/exception handling capabilities	Using preconditions and effects to specify ordering constraints.* Semantic annotation of exceptions.
Non-Functional Heterogeneous specification of provider requestor non-functional requirements	Semantic annotation of WS-Policy and WS-Agreement.
Functional Difference in functional descriptions of Web services	Annotating operations and adding preconditions/effects of the operations*
Syntax/Structure/Semantic Difference in data schemas at syntatic and semantic levels	Data mapping support by annotating inputs and outputs with ontological concepts*(XML supports syntatic interoperability
Platform/System Different operating systems, platforms	Web Service Standards (SOAP and WSDL)

* indicates support in WSDL-S and may also be supported by other SWS specifications.

Figure 5.4: Types of heterogeneity and how SWS can remedy them

upon English-language terms or as complex as expressive ontologies that use formal models such as description logics. SAWSDL service providers can choose different mapping languages, based on the modeling paradigm used. SAWSDL has so far been used to link to a variety of ontologies such as those defined in RDFS and WSML, as well as to point to diverse transformation languages such as XSLT and XSPARQL.

A functional description and automatic discovery of the service is necessary for increasing reuse in enterprises. SAWSDL's *modelReference* attribute can link operations to functional descriptions in domain models. For example, a service provider can annotate all operations that implement the Partner Interface Process (PIP) *RequestPurchaseOrder* from the *RosettaNet* standard with an identifier representing it. Using a discovery mechanism such as in METEOR-S Web Services Discovery Infrastructure (MWSDI) [Verma et al., 2005], clients can locate all services in the enterprise that implement the *RequestPurchaseOrder* PIP and reuse them as required.

The METEOR-S project has also investigated adding semantics to other Web service standards, such as Web Services Business Process Execution Language (WS-BPEL). BPEL descriptions of processes can be augmented with semantic templates to achieve runtime binding of services based on semantic discovery [Verma, 2006]. Each semantic template would use a SAWSDL description to depict the abstract functionality that a particular service partner requires. The process analysts would then use the semantic templates to find and bind partner services to the process at runtime.

Currently SAWSDL has direct support for modeling functional and data semantics. The non-functional and execution semantics can be incorporated with the help of the WS-Policy[12]

[12]http://www.w3.org/2002/ws/policy

Heterogeneities/Conflicts	Examples - conflicted elements shown in color		Suggestions/Issues in Resolving Heterogeneities
Domain Incompatibilities - *attribute level differences that arise because of using different descriptions for semantically similar attributes*			
Naming conflicts Two attributes that are semantically alike might have different names (synonyms) Two attributes that are semantically unrelated might have the same (homonyms)	**Web service 1** Student(Id#, Name) **Web service 1** Student(Id#, Name)	**Web service 2** Student(SSN, Name) **Web service 2** Book(Id#, Name)	A semantic annotation on the entities and attributes (provided by WSDL-S modelReference) will indicate their semantic similarities
Data representation conflicts Two attributes that are semantically similar might have different data types or representations	**Web service 1** Student(Id#, Name) Id# defined as a 4 digit number	**Web service 2** Student(Id#, Name) Id# defined as a 9 digit number	*Mapping WS2 Id# to WS1 Id# is easy with some additional context information while mapping in the reverse direction is most likely not possible.
Data scaling conflicts Two attributes that are semantically similar might be represented using different precisions	**Web service 1** Marks 1-100	**Web service 2** Grades A-F	*Mapping WS1 Marks to WS1 Grades is easy with some additional context information while mapping in the reverse direction is most likely not possible.
Entity Definition - *entity level differences that arise because of using different descriptions for semantically similar entities*			
Naming conflicts Semantically alike entities might have different names (synonyms) Semantically unrelated entities might have the same names (homonyms)	**Web service 1** EMPLOYEE (Id#, Name) **Web service 1** TICKET (TicketNo, MovieName)	**Web service 2** WORKER (Id#, Name) **Web service 2** TICKET (FlightNo, Arr. Airport, Dep. Airport)	A semantic annotation on the entities and attributes (provided by WSDL-S modelReferences) will indicate their semantic similarities.
Schema Isomorphism conflicts Semantically similar entities may have different number of attributes	**Web service 1** PERSON (Name, Address, HomePhone, WorkPhone)	**Web service 2** PERSON (Name, Address, Phone)	*Mapping in both directions will require some additional context information.
Abstraction Level Incompatibility - *Entity and attribute level differences that arise because two semantically similar entities or attributes are represented at different levels of abstraction*			
Generalization conflicts Semantically similar entities are represented at different levels of generalization in two Web services	**Web service 1** GRAD-STUDENT (ID, Name, Major)	**Web service 2** STUDENT (ID, Name, Major, Type)	*WS2 defines the student entity at a much general level. A mapping from WS1 to WS2 requires adding a Type element with a default "Graduate" value, while mapping in the other direction is a partial function.
Aggregation conflicts Semantically similar entities are represented at different levels of generalization in two Web services	**Web service 1** PROFESSOR (ID, Name Dept)	**Web service 2** FACULTY (ID, ProfiD, Dept)	*A set-of Professor entities is a Faculty entity. When the output of WS1 is a Professor entity, it is possible to identity the Faculty group it belongs to, but generating a mapping in the other direction is not possible.
Attribute Entity conflicts Semantically similar entities modeled as an attribute in one service and as an entity in the other	**Web service 1** COURSE (ID,Name, Semester)	**Web service 2** DEPT (Course, Sem, ...,...)	*Course modeled as an entity by WS1 is modeled as an attribute by WS2. With direction contexts, mappings can be specified in both directions.

* Interoperation between services needs transportation rules (mapping) in addition to annotation of the entities and/or attributes indicating their semantic similarity (matching).

Figure 5.5: Examples of service heterogeneities and methods to overcome them [Nagarajan et al., 2006]

framework. We also anticipate that SAWSDL will be enhanced with the ability to model preconditions, postconditions, and effects as other research efforts in SWS have explored. In the medium term, we advocate using semantics to improve SOA by enriching policy or agreement specifications that can lead to better partner selection and improved dynamic and adaptive capabilities of services and processes.

Benefits of SA-REST

Most RESTful Web services have XHTML pages that describe to users what the service does and how to invoke it. XHTML is meant to be human readable whereas WSDL is designed to be machine readable. Microformats offer a way to add semantic metadata to human readable text that enables machines to glean semantics. (See Chapters 2 and 3 for a description of annotation techniques and

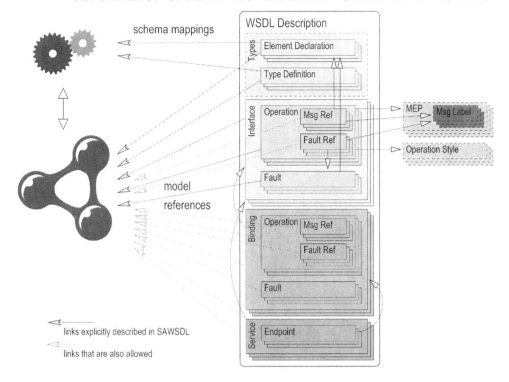

Figure 5.6: SAWSDL annotations: WSDL description to semantics (courtesy Jacek Kopecky).

technologies.) Specifically, GRDDL offers a way for the human-readable text's author to choose any microformat for annotation and specify a translation into machine-readable format; RDFa offers a way to embed RDF triples into an XML, HTML, or XHTML document. For SA-REST, we recommend using RDFa because it is a subset of RDF, extends XHTML to annotate with markups, has built-in support URIs and namespaces, and is recognized by the W3C.

In SA-REST descriptions, the semantic annotations and triples can be intermingled with the HTML or clustered together and not rendered by the Web browser. The triple's subject should be the URL at which the service is invoked; the predicate of the triple should be **sarest:input**, **sarest:output**, **sarest:operation**, **sarest:lifting**, **sarest:lowering**, or **sarest:fault**, where **sarest** is the alias to the SA-REST namespace. The triple's object should be either a URI or a URL to a resource, depending on the predicate. Figure 5.7 gives a detailed example of an SA-REST document for a Web service to search for houses on **craigslist.com**.

To build in greater flexibility, SA-REST also allows the use of GRDDL for attaching annotations. To annotate an HTML page with GRDDL for extracting RDF, the author must first embed the annotations in a microformat and add a profile attribute to the <head> tag in the HTML document. This attribute is the GRDDL profile's URL, which tells the agents coming to the HTML

```
<html xmlns:sarest="http://lsdis.cs.uga.edu/SAREST#">
. . .

    <p about="http://craiglist.org/search">
        The Logical Input of this service is an
        <span property="sarest:input">
            http://lsdis.cs.uga.edu/ont.owl#Location_Query
        </span>
        object The Logical output of this service is a list of
        <span property="sarest:output">
            http://lsdis.cs.uga.edu/ont./owl#Location
        </span>
        object This service should be invoked using an
        <span property="sarest:action">
            HTTP GET
        </span>
        <meta property="sarest:lifting" content="
            http://craiglist/org/api/lifting.xsl">
        <meta property="sarest:lowering" content="
            http://craiglist/org/api/lowering.xsl">
        <meta property="sarest:operation" content="
            http://lsdis.cs.uga.edu/
        ont.owl#Location_Search">
    </p>
```

Figure 5.7: SA-REST annotations for Craigslist search service.

page that it was annotated with GRDDL information. The final step is to add a link tag inside the head element that contains the translation document's URL. Although you can use any format to add annotations to this page, the data extracted after translation must result in RDF triples identical to those that would be generated via RDFa embedding. In other words, a page annotated with GRDDL must still produce triples whose subject is the URL used to invoke the service, whose predicate is the type of SA-REST annotation applied, and whose object is the URI or URL of the resource to which the predicate refers. The advantage of using GRDDL is that it is more flexible than RDFa, and it lets the user embed annotations in a convenient way. RDFa's advantage is that annotations are self-contained in the HTML page, so the user needs to create and maintain only a single document. In contrast, GRDDL forces the user to create two documents, the HTML page and the translation document.

Benefits of WSMO-Lite and MicroWSMO

SAWSDL does not advocate a particular ontology language or any specific vocabulary that users should adopt. In contrast, WSMO-Lite[13] provides a minimal RDFS ontology and a simple methodology for expressing the four types of semantic annotations for WSDL services using the three types of SAWSDL hooks. WSMO-Lite offers two mechanisms for representing functional semantics, namely simple taxonomies and more expressive preconditions and effects. Whenever more expres-

---

[13]http://www.w3.org/Submission/2010/SUBM-WSMO-Lite-20100823/

sivity is necessary, WSMO-Lite offers the possibility to enrich functional classification with logical expressions defining conditions that need to hold prior to service execution, and capturing changes that the service will carry out on the world. Nonfunctional semantics in WSMO-Lite are represented using external ontologies capturing nonfunctional properties such as security aspects, the quality of service, and price. Behavioral semantics describe how the client should communicate with a service. Clients are required to use the existing functional annotations (classifications, conditions, and effects) over the entire service and the internal operations to figure out in which order to invoke them. The information model captures the semantics of the data exchanged between a service and its clients. WSMO-Lite relies on external ontologies for capturing information models.

Discovering services, handling heterogeneous data, and creating service compositions are predominantly manual and tedious tasks because of lack of machine-processable descriptions. MicroWSMO is a microformat supporting the semantic annotation of RESTful services and Web APIs in order to better support their automatic discovery, composition, and invocation. MicroWSMO builds upon hRESTS (HTML for RESTful services) which enables the creation of machine-processable Web API descriptions. It provides a number of HTML classes that allow one to structure APIs descriptions by identifying services, operations, methods, inputs, outputs, and addresses. With the hRESTS structure in place, HTML service descriptions can be annotated further by including pointers to the semantics of the service, operations, and data manipulated. To this end, MicroWSMO extends hRESTS with three additional properties, namely, model, lifting, and lowering that are borrowed from SAWSDL and have the same semantics as explained earlier. Although not strictly necessary, MicroWSMO adopts the WSMO-Lite ontology as the reference ontology for annotating RESTful services semantically. By doing so, both WSDL services and RESTful services annotated with WSMO-Lite and MicroWSMO respectively can be treated similarly. See the following listing for an example of a MicroWSMO annotation.

```
<div class="service" id="s1">
  <h1>happenr API</h1>
  <a rel="model" href="http://example.com/events/getEvents">
    <span class="label">Happenr </span>has two main methods to call
    "getEvents" and . .
  </a>
  <p>All operations should be directed at http://happenr.3scale.net/</p>
  <h2>Example usage</h2>
  <span class="address">
    http://happenr.3scale.ws/webservices/getEvents.php?user_key=xxx
  </span>
  <p>where the userkey is the key issues with the signup you made.</p>
  <div class="operation" id="op1"><h2>
    <span class="label">getEvents
    </span>Method</h2>
    <span class="input">
    <h3>
        <a rel="model"
           href="http://example.com/data/onto.owl#Username">username</a>
      (<a rel="lowering"
           href="http://example.com/data/event.xsparql">lowering</a>)
    </h3>
```

```
<p>Your username that you received from Happenr </p>
<h3 >
    <a rel="model"
        href="http://example.com/data/onto.owl#Password">password<a>
    (<a rel="lowering"
        href="http://example.com/data/event.xsparql">lowering </a>)
</h3>
<p>Your password that you received from Happenr in order to query this webservice
</p>
```

For a detailed description of the SWS tools, see [Pedrinaci et al., 2011].

5.4 EXAMPLE APPLICATIONS OF SEMANTICALLY ANNOTATED WEB SERVICES

SWS applications are typically structured around the following four layers [Pedrinaci et al., 2011] (see Figure 5.8):

- *Legacy system layer*: Consists of the existing data sources and IT systems available from each of the organizations involved in the integrated application.

- *Services abstraction layer*: Exposes (micro-) functionalities of the legacy systems as Web services, abstracting from the hardware and software platforms.

- *Semantic Web service layer*: Sets up an application based on a set of application-specific SWS descriptions provided. These descriptions are typically centrally stored within some repository for easy querying and retrieval through a more or less advanced discovery or service matchmaking machinery.

- *Presentation layer*: Consists of a Web application accessible through a standard Web browser. The possible actions presented depend on the underlying services available. Typically, input and output data are directly gathered from and presented to the user based on some semantic representation such as RDF(S), OWL, or WSML.

As part of the SWS Challenge, we demonstrated how SAWSDL, with different types of semantics, can be used to model and successfully implement a fairly complex scenario [Verma, 2006]. Specifically, we demonstrated this approach's utility in a supply-chain scenario in which we created a supply-chain process using a WS-Process; SAWSDL descriptions captured the required suppliers—semantic templates. The system was then able to choose optimal suppliers for each part at runtime. This work also showed how using SAWSDL descriptions of services along with the WS-Policy standard can help model a service's runtime execution and exception behavior, and how that model can adapt the process to logical exceptions such as delays in ordered goods.

Using semantics to integrate and coordinate mashups gives us smashups (semantic mashups) [Lathem et al., 2007]. Annotations give smashups the ability to know more about a service's inputs

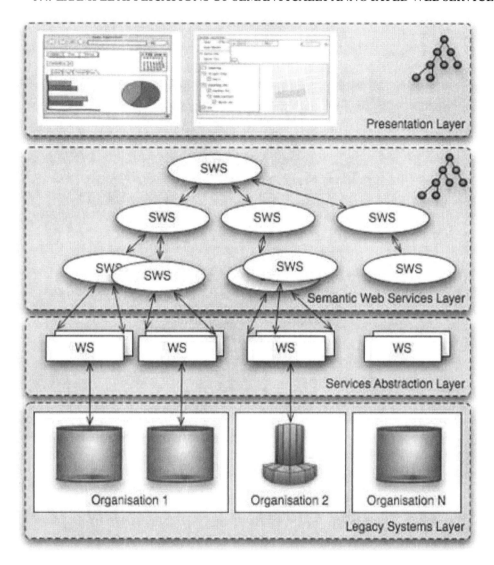

Figure 5.8: Typical architecture of SWS-based applications [Pedrinaci et al., 2011] (copyright © IEEE, with permission).

and outputs and what the service does, which facilitates data mediation. Figure 5.9 shows a typical smashup architecture that uses two RESTful Web services (a movie finder and a mapping service). The key component of this architecture is the proxy server, which hosts the smashup editor, and the ontologies that capture the semantics enabling reasoning and data mediation. Users can also

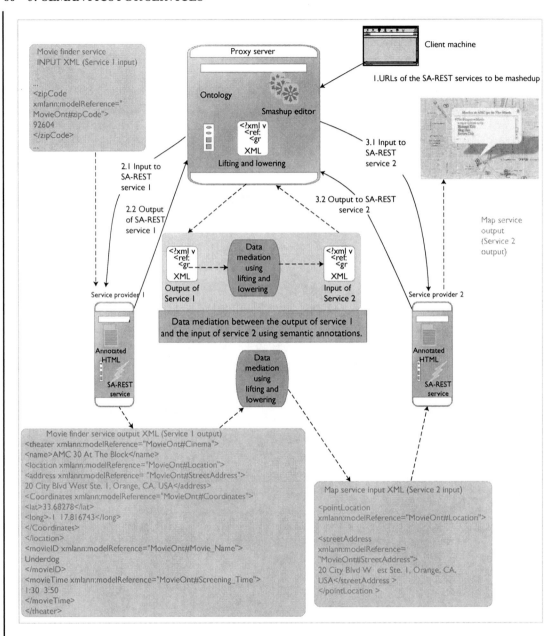

Figure 5.9: Mashup architecture. User query (1) results in invocation of service1 (2.1 and 2.2); data mediation (DM1 and DM2) of output XML from service 1(2.2) maps the input of service 2; and the proxy server is the container for the smashup editor, ontologies, and data mediation rules (as XSLT) [Sheth et al., 2007] (copyright © IEEE, with permission).

specify data mediation using the principles of lifting and lowering with the XSLTs that capture these mediation rules. In this example, the user sends a zip code object to the movie-finder service. The proxy server extracts the location information from the output of the movie-finder service and sends it as an input to the mapping service. Once the mapping service returns the map canvas, the rest of the information about the movie title and the timings are displayed in the map. Additional discussions on the role of semantics in the broader context of services science that encompasses Web services as well as organizational issues can be found in [Lathem et al., 2007, Martin and Domingue, 2007a,b].

An application of SA-REST in the domain of bioinformatics is exemplified by the Kino system [Ranabahu et al., 2011a]. Kino tools have been adapted for annotating bioinformatics documents using terms from NCBO (National Center for Biomedical Ontology) ontologies,[14] and subsequently indexing and searching them flexibly. NCBO currently hosts 260 ontologies containing nearly 5 million terms. For example, GO (Gene Ontology) annotations produce high quality, species and gene product metadata in a format that can be used in high-throughput experiments. Various steps to perform genome sequencing are encapsulated as Web services, and the annotations and their synonyms can be used to search through a service catalog such as BioCatalogue, importing the relevant service description to a composer tool. The manual annotation tool is available as a browser plugin, index is built using Apache SOLR, and search uses JavaScript-driven Web UI. NCBO provide RESTful APIs. See Figure 5.10 for overall architecture and Figure 5.11 for search interface.

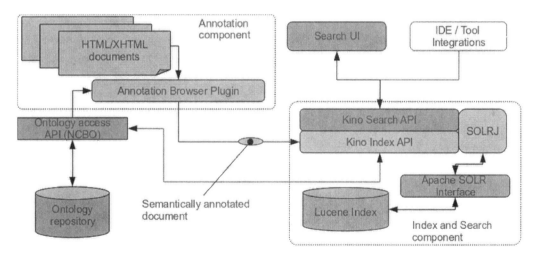

Figure 5.10: Kino Architecture for annotation, index, and search. Annotation is performed manually via bowser-plugin. Indexer indexes the document taking into account its attributes and synonyms of the annotations, to facilitate search [Ranabahu et al., 2011a].

[14]http://www.bioontology.org

Welcome to Kino Faceted Index and Search Engine

Figure 5.11: Snapshot of Kino Faceted Index and Search Engine [Ranabahu et al., 2011a].

SWS technologies have also been applied in the eGovernment domain [Gugliotta et al., 2008]. The use cases show how SWS technology provides an infrastructure in which new services can be added, discovered, and composed continually, and the organization processes automatically updated to reflect new forms of cooperation. The two compelling use cases considered in the eGovernment domain were: Change of Circumstances and the Emergency Management System. The first application illustrates how Web services and ontologies can be leveraged in order to support a seamless integration and interaction within and between governmental administrative organizations to automatically handle the change of a citizen situation. The second application illustrated support for emergency planning and management personnel by retrieving, filtering, and presenting data from a variety of legacy systems to deal with a specified hazardous situation. It emphasized the dynamics of SWS technologies by showing how systems can dynamically and transparently choose and orchestrate specific services in order to better deal with the situation at hand. Although the two examples are based on WSMO and IRS-III as the specific execution environments, most of the techniques and solutions are portable to different modeling and execution frameworks.

In the long term, we hope to see a pervasive impact of semantics through all the states of service and process life cycle, encompassing publication, discovery, orchestration, composition, and dynamic configuration, ultimately leading to adaptive Web services and processes. Machine-processable annotations and service specifications will be critical for scalability and widespread use of service mashups.

CHAPTER 6

Semantics for Sensor Data

Sensors are distributed across the globe leading to an avalanche of data about our environment. According to a 2009 projection from Nokia [2008], there are 40+ billion mobile sensors, 4 billion mobile devices, and 1.1 billion PCs. According to an IBM study [IBM, 2012], 2.5 quintillion bytes of data are created daily and 90% of the data today were generated in the last two years. According to Evans [2011], 25 billion devices will be connected to the Internet by 2015 and 50 billion by 2020. With their enormous growth rate, sensor data will trump other types of data in a short time. It is possible today to utilize networks of sensors to detect and identify a multitude of observations, from simple phenomena to complex events and situations. The lack of integration and communication between these networks, however, often isolates important data streams and intensifies the existing problem of too much data and not enough information, knowledge, and insight. With a view to addressing this problem, the Semantic Sensor Web (SSW) [Sheth et al., 2008b] proposes that sensor data be annotated with semantic metadata that will both increase interoperability and provide contextual information essential for situational awareness. We explore (i) the nature of machine sensor data, (ii) the benefits of augmenting sensor data with semantics, (iii) the domain-specific and spatio-temporal problems to be addressed for realizing semantic sensor networks and processing data obtained from them, (iv) the role of Semantic Web technology in the organization and architecture of query and decision support system that can be built on top of semantic sensor networks foundation, and standardization efforts underway to make sensor-related data and sensor observations widely available and usable, and (v) potential areas of application. In fact, the role of semantics discussed here is applicable to describing sensors, controllers, and actuators embedded in physical objects that are part of fast emerging Internet of Things (IoT). For example, Linked Sensor/Stream Middleware (`http://lsm.deri.ie/`) provides a platform for aggregating and annotating real world sensed data using Semantic Web technologies [Phuoc et al., 2011]. Spitfire project (`http://spitfire-project.eu/`) is developing applications that span and integrate the Internet and the embedded world.

> *The most profound technologies are those that disappear. They weave themselves into the fabric of everyday life until they are indistinguishable from it.*
>
> *Weiser's (1991) Vision of Calm Technology*

> *Small computers would be embedded in everyday objects around us and, using wireless connections, would respond to our presence, desires and needs without being actively manipulated. This network of mobile and fixed devices would do things for us automatically and so invisibly that we would notice only their effects.*
>
> *Want's (2004) elaboration on Weiser's vision*

6.1   NATURE OF SENSOR DATA

In recent years, sensors have been increasingly adopted by a diverse array of disciplines, such as meteorology for weather forecasting and wild-fire detection (http://www.met.utah.edu/mesowest/), civic planning for traffic management (http://www.buckeyetraffic.org/), satellite imaging for earth and space observation (http://vast.uah.edu/), medical sciences for patient care using biometric sensors (http://www.liebertonline.com/doi/abs/10.1089/109350703322682531), and homeland security for radiation and biochemical detection at ports (http://www.msnbc.msn.com/id/8092280). The rapid development and deployment of sensor technology involves many different types of sensors, both remote and in situ, with diverse capabilities such as range, modality, and maneuverability. Embedded networked sensing involves untethered, networked devices tightly coupled to the physical world, to monitor and interact with it. In spite of the potential of sensor networks to form the basis for our understanding of complex events and situations, they have remained largely untapped because of lack of meaningful integration (also termed fusion), abstraction, and interpretation of sensor data streams.

6.2   ROLE OF SEMANTICS IN SENSOR NETWORKS: SPACE, TIME, AND THEME

Sensors' encoding of observed phenomena are often in binary or proprietary formats; therefore, metadata play an essential role in managing sensor data. To understand the role and impact of sensor data, they should be situated in its environment. To interpret sensor data properly, we should (at least) specify the kind of data sensed in terms of magnitude and unit of measurement, and to assimilate their full impact it is useful to provide contextual information such as the location of the sensor and the time at which the sensor data were obtained (see Figure 6.1). That is, a semantically rich sensor network should provide spatial, temporal, and thematic information essential for discovering, analyzing, and contextually interpreting sensor data [Sheth and Perry, 2008].

Spatial metadata provide information regarding the sensor location and data, in terms of either a geographical reference system, local reference, or named location. Local reference is especially useful when a sensor is attached to a moving object such as a car or airplane. While the sensor's location is constantly changing, its location can be statically determined relative to the moving object. In addition, data from remote sensors, such as video and images from cameras and satellites, require complex spatial models to represent the field of view being monitored, which is distinct from the sensor's location. Temporal metadata provides information regarding the time instants or intervals when the sensor data were captured. Thematic metadata describe a real-world state, such as objects or events, from sensor observations. Every discipline contains unique domain-specific information, such as concepts describing weather phenomena, structural integrity values of buildings, or biomedical events representing a patient's health status. Thematic metadata can be created or derived by several means, such as sensor data analysis, extraction of textual descriptions, or social tagging. The context provided by the metadata is critical to assess the nature of the situation the sensors observe. For

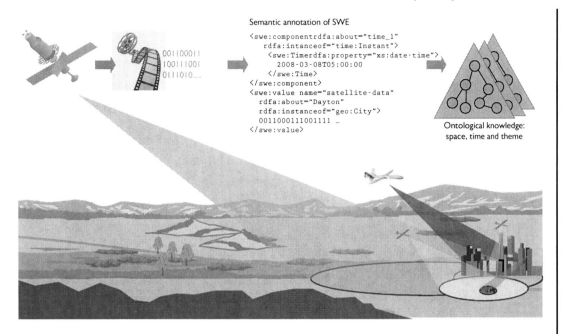

Semantic annotation of SWE

```
<swe:componentrdfa:about="time_1"
   rdfa:intanceof="time:Instant">
   <swe:Timerdfa:property="xs:date-time">
      2008-03-08T05:00:00
   </swe:Time>
</swe:component>
<swe:value name="satellite-data"
   rdfa:about="Dayton"
   rdfa:instanceof="geo:City">
   0011000111001111 …
</swe:value>
```

Ontological knowledge:
space, time and theme

Figure 6.1: From natural phenomena to raw sensor data to semantics. [Sheth et al., 2008b] (copyright © IEEE, with permission)

example, a temperature of 105 degree Fahrenheit has different implications depending on whether the context is human body or bath water. Furthermore, spatio-temporal metadata can assist with "thematic registration."

Whereas the languages provided by the Open Geospatial Consortium (OGC) Sensor Web Enablement (SWE) provide annotations for simple spatial and temporal concepts such as *spatial coordinate* and *timestamp*, more abstract concepts, such as *spatial region*, *temporal interval*, or any domain-specific thematic entity, would benefit from an ontological representation's expressiveness. Consider, for example, the semantics of a query about weather information at a particular time and place. The type of weather condition being sought could be a simple phenomenon, such as a single temperature reading, or a complex one, such as a tsunami. The location type within the query could be a single coordinate location, a spatial region within a bounding-box, or a named location such as a park or school. The semantics of the time interval specified by the query could be about weather conditions that fall *within* the time interval, *contain* the time interval, or *overlap* with the time interval. The type of metadata necessary to answer the queries listed requires knowledge of the situation the sensors observe. Such knowledge can be represented in ontologies and used to annotate and reason over sensor data to answer complex queries.

To emphasize the need to integrate spatio-temporal reasoning with sensor data processing in a rich information system, consider the following queries in the context of smart homes and smart buildings [Thirunarayan and Pschorr, 2009]:

- What is the current average temperature in the building?

- How many motion detector sensors are present in the 4th floor?

- What was the average humidity in the areas with temperature > 25F last week?

Similarly, consider how to bridge the gap between a seismic (vibration) sensor data containing latitude/longitude information and time of observation, and the query that requests the number of earthquakes in United States last year. Sensor fusion problem goes one step further by requiring multiple sensor data to build evidence for a real-world event, such as using temperature, humidity, and pressure data to forecast weather.

Geo-spatio-temporal aspects have much wider applicability, beyond sensor network applications, as exemplified by the following queries in the context of terrorist activities:

- How many car bombs exploded near Tel Aviv in the last three months?

- Was there an insurgency incident within 30 miles of the Green Zone (in Baghdad) in March 2006?

Consider another example that involves the detonation detected by the Scripps Institution of Oceanography at the University of California as described by Space.com (2001). A new array of infrasound sensors, designed to detect the underground detonation of a nuclear weapon, registered an explosion in the direction of the Pacific Ocean on April 23, 2001. After collaborating with other monitoring stations and comparing their data, the researchers determined that it was a meteorite detonating in the atmosphere. Ideally, we might wish to connect all such sensors into a semantic sensor network. When such an event happens again, the semantic sensor network would respond by firing an alert. That alert might cause the automatic classification of the sensed phenomena by aggregating and fusing data from multiple monitoring stations. The temporal differences for the event among the monitoring stations, as well as the direction of travel of the shockwave might be combined in such a way as to produce a new composite alert classifying the sensed phenomena as a meteorite or a nuclear explosion with a given degree of certainty.

Today, many sensor networks and their applications employ a brute force approach to collecting and analyzing sensor data. Such an approach often wastes valuable energy and computational resources by unnecessarily tasking sensors and generating observations of minimal use. It is possible to exploit background semantic knowledge and models of events being monitored to determine what aspects of the environment to focus our attention on while collecting and interpreting raw sensor data. In fact, *such an approach to machine perception holds the key to simultaneously minimizing the amount of information needed for perception and enabling graceful degradation of perception when faced with incomplete information.*

6.3   CREATION OF SEMANTIC METADATA: MODELS AND ANNOTATIONS

One of the early obstacles to developing and deploying large-scale Sensor Web was the lack of standards. The Sensor Web Enablement (SWE) Working Group of the Open Geospatial Consortium (OGC) has tried to address this problem by developing a number of candidate specifications for disseminating information related to sensor data, sensing devices, and sensor services [Botts et al., 2008, Thirunarayan and Pschorr, 2009]:

- *Observations & Measurements (O&M)* - Standard models and XML Schema for encoding observations and measurements from a sensor, both archived and real time.

- *Sensor Model Language (SensorML)* - Standard models and XML Schema for describing sensors systems and processes; provides information needed for discovery of sensors, location of sensor observations, processing of low-level sensor observations, and listing of taskable properties.

- *Transducer Model Language (TransducerML or TML)* - The conceptual model and XML Schema for describing transducers and supporting real-time streaming of data to and from sensor systems.

- *Sensor Observations Service (SOS)* - Standard Web service interface for requesting, filtering, and retrieving observations and sensor system information. This is the intermediary between a client and an observation repository or near real-time sensor channel.

- *Sensor Planning Service (SPS)* - Standard Web service interface for requesting user-driven acquisitions and observations. This is the intermediary between a client and a sensor collection management environment.

- *Sensor Alert Service (SAS)* - Standard Web service interface for publishing and subscribing to alerts from sensors.

- *Web Notification Services (WNS)* - Standard Web service interface for asynchronous delivery of messages or alerts from SAS and SPS Web services and other elements of service workflows.

Web applications based on these standards enable sensor discovery, evaluation of sensor characteristics based on their published descriptions, communication with sensor system to retrieve the characteristics of the sensor platform, determine its state and location, tasking commands to the sensor or its platform, and access to its data. These standards provide annotations for the expression of simple concepts such as location coordinates, timestamp, and sensor specification. However, to provide the ability for rich semantic reasoning over the sensed data, more expressive annotations are necessary. Integration with ontologies would provide the benefit of additional annotations for abstract concepts, such as temporal relationships, geographic region, and domain-specific themes.

The SSW is a framework for providing enhanced meaning for sensor observations so as to enable situation awareness. It is accomplished by adding semantic annotations to existing standard sensor languages of the SWE. These annotations provide more meaningful descriptions and enhanced access to sensor data than SWE alone, and they act as a linking mechanism to bridge the gap between the primarily syntactic XML-based metadata standards of the SWE and the RDF/OWL-based metadata standards of the Semantic Web. In association with semantic annotation, ontologies, and rules play an important role in SSW for interoperability, analysis, and reasoning over heterogeneous multimodal sensor data.

6.3.1   SEMANTIC ANNOTATION

Many languages can be used for annotating sensor data, such as RDFa, XLink, and SAWSDL (Semantic Annotations for WSDL and XML Schema). The following simple example shows a timestamp encoded in O&M and semantically annotated with RDFa (see Chapter 3, Section 3.3.3). The timestamp's semantic annotation describes an instance of *time:Instant* (here, *time* is the namespace for an OWL-Time ontology, which is an ontology for describing the temporal content of web pages and the temporal properties of Web Services):

> < swe:component rdfa:about="time_1" rdfa:intanceof="time:Instant">
>
> < swe:Time rdfa:property="xs:date-time">2008-0308T05:00:00</swe:Time >
>
> < / swe:component >

This example generates two RDF triples. The first triple, time_1 rdf:type time:Instant, describes *time_1* as an instance of *time:Instant* (subject is *time_1*, predicate is *rdf:type*, object is *time:Instant*). The second triple, time_1 xs:date-time "2008-03-08T05:00:00," describes a datatype property of *time_1* specifying the time as a literal value (subject is *time_1*, predicate is *xs:date-time*, object is *"2008-03-08T05:00:00"*). This example illustrates the simple mechanics of embedding semantics in an XML document using RDFa. In summary, semantically annotating SWE languages enables software applications to "understand" and formally reason over sensor data consistently, coherently, and accurately.

6.3.2   ONTOLOGIES

Broadly speaking, we can classify ontologies used in the SSW context along three types of semantics associated with sensor data—*spatial*, *temporal*, and *thematic*—in addition to ontological models representing the sensors domain.

Several initiatives have helped to build relevant ontologies within various communities, such as the National Institute of Standards and Technology (http://www.nist.gov/), the W3C, and the OGC. NIST initiated a project titled "Sensor Standards Harmonization" to develop a common sensor ontology based on the existing standards within the sensors domain, including IEEE 1451, ANSI N42.42, the CBRN Data Model, and the OGC developed the SWE languages. Several efforts were dedicated to design expressive geospatial ontology, including the W3C Geospatial Incubator Group (http://www.w3.org/2005/Incubator/geo/) and the Geographic Markup Language Ontology (http://loki.cae.drexel.edu/~wbs/ontology/ogc-gml.htm) of the OGC. OWL-Time (http://www.w3.org/TR/owl-time/), a W3C-recommended ontology based on temporal calculus, provides descriptions of temporal concepts such as *instant* and *interval*, which supports defining interval queries such as *within*, *contains*, and *overlaps* [Hobbs and Pan, 2004]. Domain-specific ontologies that model various sensor-related fields such as weather and oceanography (http://www.oostethys.org/) are also necessary to provide semantic descriptions of thematic entities. We envision a registry of domain-specific ontologies for the SSW, similar to those at the National Center for Biomedical Ontologies[1] that will catalog and provide services related to sharing and use of broad variety of ontologies in sensor applications. Figure 6.2 shows a subset of concepts and their relations from a suite of ontologies in SSW modeling the weather domain.

Orthogonal to the spatio-temporal-thematic ontologies discussed so far, an ontology of perception, called *Intellego,* was developed to interpret sensor data on the Web using background knowledge. This approach is *efficient* because it minimizes resource usage by focusing attention on contextually relevant data and *effective* because it degrades gracefully in the presence of incomplete information, to achieve "semantic scalability."

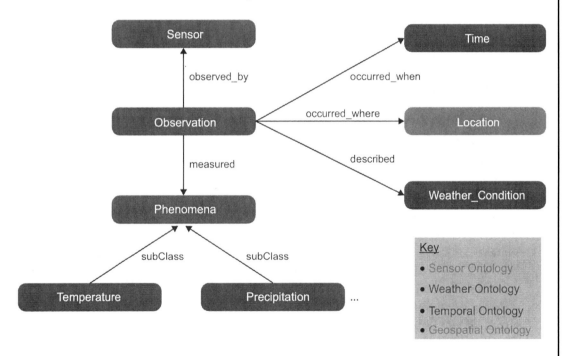

Figure 6.2: Subset of important concepts and relations in SSW. [Sheth et al., 2008b]

---

[1]http://www.bioontology.org/

6.3.3   SEMANTIC SENSOR NETWORK ONTOLOGY

Sensors are anything that can estimate or calculate the value of a phenomenon, so a device or computational process or combination could play the role of a sensor. The representation of a sensor in the ontology links together what it measures (the domain phenomena), the physical sensor (the device), and its functions and processing (the models). The ontology can be used for a focus on any (or a combination) of a number of perspectives:

- A sensor perspective, with a focus on what it senses and how;

- A data or observation perspective, with a focus on observations and related metadata;

- A system perspective, with a focus on systems of sensors; or,

- A feature and property perspective, with a focus on features, properties of them, and what can sense those properties.

Specifically, the ontology provides modules containing classes and properties that can be used to represent particular aspects of a sensor or its observations: for example, sensors, observations, features of interest, the process of sensing (i.e., how a sensor operates and observes), how sensors are deployed or attached to platforms, the measuring capabilities of sensors, as well as the environmental and survival properties of sensors in particular environments. See [Lefort et al., 2011] for detailed examples.

6.3.4   RULE-BASED REASONING

To derive additional knowledge from semantically annotated sensor data, it is necessary to define and use rules. To demonstrate rules application and rule-based reasoning, we can use Semantic Web Rule Language (SRWL)-based rules defined over OWL ontologies to deduce new ontological assertions from known instances. SWRL (http://www.w3.org/SWRL) has been proposed by the W3C as a standard rule language in the Semantic Web; it is based on OWL and uses *antecedent* → *consequent* structure to define rules. Its primary advantage is that it seamlessly incorporates rules into an OWL ontology schema while providing enhanced application-specific expressivity. To illustrate abstraction of weather phenomena values to weather features in SSW, we can specify rules that map temperature and precipitation values provided by a group of sensors explicitly to possible road conditions. For example, if the temperature is less than 32 degrees Fahrenheit and it is raining, then the roads are *potentially icy*. Note that the rules can be made more succinct by supporting types in the rule language.

6.3.5   QUERYING SEMANTIC SENSOR WEB

An SSN database can be queried to retrieve information about the structure and the nature of sensors, their locations and observations, potentially as a function of time. Responses to such *basic queries* are grounded in the explicit information about the sensors available in the database. Sensor data can be

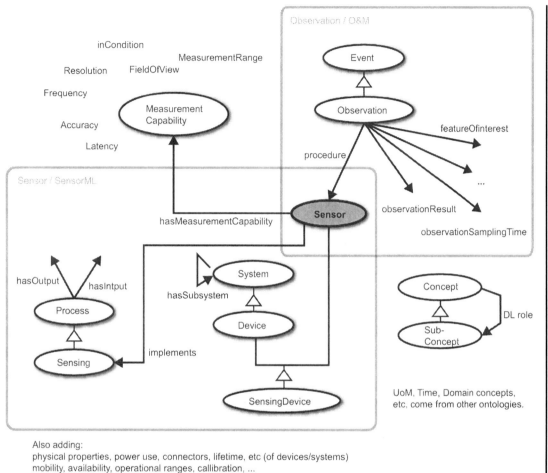

Figure 6.3: W3C Semantic Sensor Network Ontology [Compton et al., 2012].

made more intelligible (such as in the context of a decision support system) by enabling *semantics-rich symbolic queries* with natural space-related and time-related vocabulary, such as references to geographical locations, relative vs. absolute time points, various time intervals, and by enabling *aggregation queries* for synthesizing aggregate information such as total, average, and maximum. In a number of situations, it may be necessary to trigger an alert or an action when a specific real-world state is reached or is prevailing. The observers need to register/subscribe to an event to be published, and will be alerted or notified asynchronously when the event occurs.

We may characterize the former application as *data collection*, while the latter application as *alarm monitoring for action*. Typically, the former may be used for informational purposes (such as regularly reporting building temperature), while the latter may be used for event reporting to troubleshooting (such as in battlefield surveillance application where "events-of-interest" are reported to the gateway computer). In a dynamic environment, one may add a third activity—*object tracking*—that requires continuous data collection and mapping between snapshots taken at different times. The long-term vision of SSW is to be able to develop a system that can relate and reason with various entities and events, and potentially predict future occurrences of events or involvements of entities, by representing and reasoning with entities (organizations, persons), events (themes), space (geography), and time (duration).

6.4   EXAMPLES OF SEMANTIC APPLICATIONS

As a proof of concept, two prototype applications were implemented.

The first involves YouTube videos encoded in SensorML and semantically annotated with concepts from an OWL-Time ontology [Henson et al., 2007]. All videos in the prototype originate from Ohio State Patrol in-dash cameras that contain temporal information within the video frames. The temporal metadata are extracted using an open source optical character recognition (OCR) engine called Tesseract (`http://code.google.com/p/tesseract-ocr/`). Using this semantic metadata, we can retrieve videos by using semantic temporal concepts such as *within*, *contains*, or *overlaps* when querying with an interval of time. We can position the videos retrieved from a query onto a Google Map and play them from within an information window. Figure 6.4 shows a screenshot of the interface for this SSW prototype application. In general, images taken with GPS-enabled cameras that automatically generate spatial coordinates and time-stamp metadata, Web-based photo album with manually annotated location information, user-generated geospatial metadata created with geo-tagging vocabularies such as geoRSS, or Web mashups created using public map services are becoming common-place. These real-world scenarios illustrate the application of Semantic Web data with spatial and temporal flavor.

The second prototype is an SOS, as specified by the SWE, which uses the SSW framework to enable complex queries over weather data. We refer to this type of service as a *Semantic Sensor Observation Service* (SemSOS) [Henson et al., 2009]. As described earlier, SOS is a service for requesting, filtering, and retrieving observations and sensor system information. SOS acts as an intermediary between a client and an observation repository or near real-time sensor channel. Our application implements a SemSOS weather service that uses weather readings available at `http://www.BuckeyeTraffic.org`, a website maintained by the Ohio Department of Transportation. BuckeyeTraffic provides road and weather observations from more than 200 sensors deployed along Ohio interstate highways. Our application collects and uses data including temperatures of the air, surface, subsurface, and dew point, as well as wind speed, wind direction, and precipitation. We collected and stored such data for one month at 10-second reading intervals. We then converted the data to O&M and SML representation formats and semantically annotated these documents with spatial, temporal, and weather ontological concepts. Figure 6.5 shows the overall system architecture.

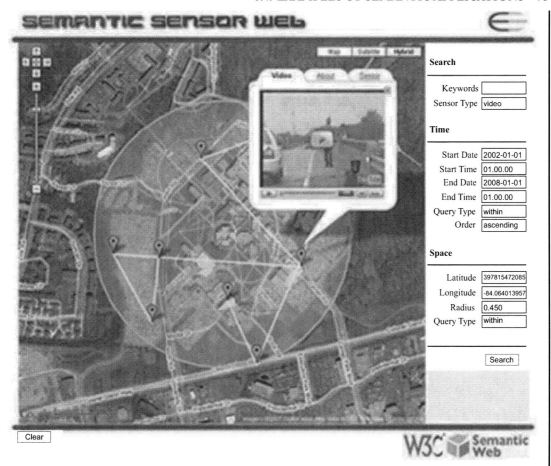

Figure 6.4: A semantic mashup with ability to show videos that capture. [Sheth et al., 2008b] (copyright © IEEE, with permission)

By leveraging SSW semantic annotations, we can fluently execute complex queries over simple weather readings. For example, it supports direct querying for human comprehensible weather features such as freezing or blizzard conditions at a particular time and place. The freezing query requires only a temperature sensor and a rule specifying that any temperature less than 32 degrees Fahrenheit constitutes a freezing condition. The blizzard query, on the other hand, requires three sensor types—temperature, wind, and precipitation. In fact, we can describe the blizzard condition as a composition of several simple (single sensor) conditions including freezing, high winds, and snowing. Complex queries of this type require semantic annotation and reasoning over sensor data.

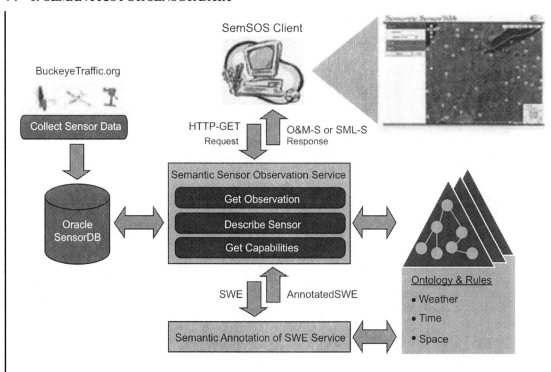

Figure 6.5: Semantic Sensor Observation Service (SemSOS) Architecture [Henson et al., 2009]
.

To derive additional knowledge from semantically annotated sensor observations, we currently use the general purpose rule engine from the Jena Semantic Web Framework (`http://jena.sourceforge.net/`). We illustrate this with an example of inference through rules in Sem-SOS [Henson et al., 2009].

The following set of RDF triples represents data about a wind speed observation.

```
om:windspeed_1 rdf:type w:WindSpeedObservation .
om:windspeed_1 om:samplingTime om:time{\_}1 .
om:windspeed_1 om:observationLocation om:location{\_}1 .
om:windspeed_1 om:result om:result{\_}1 .
om:result_1 om:value ''37'' .
om:result_1 om:uom w:MPH .
```

From this set of RDF triples we can infer that observation w:windspeed_1 can also be defined as an instance of class w:HighWindSpeedObservation. This new assertion is added to the original set of RDF triples.

```
om:windspeed_1 rdf:type w:HighWindSpeedObservation .
```

The rule used to generate this new knowledge, titled *HighWindSpeedObservationRule*, is specified below in the Jena rule syntax.

[*HighWindSpeedObservationRule*:

```
(?s_obs rdf:type w:WindSpeedObservation)
(?s_obs om:samplingTime ?time)
(?s_obs om:observationLocation ?location)
(?s_obs om:result ?result)
(?result om:uom w:MPH)
(?result om:value ?value)
greaterThan(?value 35)
⟶
(?s_obs rdf:type w:HighWindSpeedObservation)]
```

A low visibility observation (w:LowVisibilityObservation) is deduced similarly, and together with a snowfall precipitation observation (w:SnowfallObservation) we can infer a blizzard event (w:Blizzard) at the same time and location. The rule used to generate this new knowledge is titled *BlizzardObservationRule*.

[*BlizzardObservationRule*:

```
(?s_obs rdf:type w:HighWindSpeedObservation)
(?s_obs om:samplingTime ?time)
(?s_obs om:observationLocation ?location)
(?v_obs rdf:type w:LowVisibilityObservation)
(?v_obs om:samplingTime ?time)
(?v_obs om:observationLocation ?location)
(?p_obs rdf:type w:SnowfallObservation)
(?p_obs om:samplingTime ?time)
(?p_obs om:observationLocation ?location)
makeTemp(?blizzard)
⟶
(?blizzard rdf:type w:Blizzard)
(?blizzard om:eventTime ?time)
(?blizzard om:eventLocation ?location)
(?w_obs om:featureOfInterest ?blizzard)
(?v_obs om:featureOfInterest ?blizzard)
(?p_obs om:featureOfInterest ?blizzard)]
```

Note that the makeTemp(?blizzard) function in the body of the rule generates a new instance in the knowledge base. Subsequently, we supply this instance of om:Blizzard with relations in the head of the rule. In this example, such relations include rdf:type, om:eventTime, om:eventLocation, and om:featureOfInterest. The final set of RDF triples is shown below (ellipses used to truncate set of triples, and new triples in bold).

```
om:windspeed_1 rdf:type w:WindSpeedObservation .
om:windspeed_1 om:samplingTime om:time_1 .
om:windspeed_1 om:observationLocation om:location_1 .
......
om:windspeed_1 rdf:type w:HighWindSpeedObservation .
om:visibility_1 rdf:type w:VisibilityObservation .
......
om:visibility_1 rdf:type w:LowVisibilityObservation .
om:precipitation_1 rdf:type w:SnowfallObservation .
...
om:blizzard_1 rdf:type w:Blizzard .
om:blizzard_1 om:samplingTime om:time_1 .
om:blizzard_1 om:observationLocation om:location_1 .
om:windspeed_1 om:featureOfInterest om:blizzard_1 .
om:visibility_1 om:featureOfInterest om:blizzard_1 .
om:precipitation_1 om:featureOfInterest om:blizzard_1.
```

In this manner, we can infer features within the environment, of a particular type, at a specific time and place, and then generate om:featureOfInterest relations between the original observations and the new features. These new om:featureOfInterest relationships can be used to query for high-level feature concepts in SemSOS.

As explained, by incorporating OGC and W3C standardization efforts into SSW, we can provide an environment for enhanced query and reasoning within the sensor domain. We see great potential for the SSW in many different domains, including weather forecasting, oceanography, biometrics, and EventWeb [Jain, 2008].

SSN Ontology has been used in a number of applications: (1) The Channel Coastal Observatory (CCO) is a well-used sensor network data source in the Solent region (in Southern UK). This network consists of a large number of deployed nodes with sensors, which, when associated with an appropriate spatial model, can detect if a flood is ongoing or likely in the near future throughout the Solent region. If this information can be combined with additional data sets pertaining to assets and ecological services, the impact of flood may be minimized by providing additional details during an emergency response and planning mode. For example, they may want to find all the observations related to weather conditions and tide information available in a specific bounding box (or in a specific region) and obtained in the last 24 hours, and to link them to the economic assets that could be affected by a potential flood event. Here, sensor and other data assets are described with respect to the SSN ontology. (2) In the context of device discovery and selection, the sensor manufacturers and buyers can benefit from subscribing to SSN ontology which can capture information about sensor capabilities, performance, and the conditions in which it can be used. This can be defining accuracy, precision, drift, sensitivity, selectivity, measurement range, detection limit, response time, frequency and latency. (3) SSN Ontology can be applied to extend the work done on sensor discovery, linked sensor data, and sensor data provenance [Pschorr et al., 2010]. There has been a drive recently to make sensor data accessible on the Web. However, because of the vast number of environmental sensors, finding relevant sensors on the Web is a non-trivial challenge. This approach for discovering sensors uses a standard service interface to query Linked Sensor Data, a semantic sensor network middleware that includes a sensor registry and a sensor discovery service that extends the OGC SWE.[2]

In fact, SSW will play an increasingly important role in the development of cyber-physical systems [Thirunarayan and Pschorr, 2009]. A sensor node is a low-cost (and typically battery-powered) device that integrates micro-sensing, onboard processing, and wireless communication, and acts as a bridge between the physical world and the digital world. A collection of networked sensors can be made to work collaboratively for seismic structure response monitoring, marine microorganisms tracking, contaminant transport and environment monitoring, battlefield monitoring for tactical situation awareness and decision making, medical monitoring and drug delivery, search and rescue, disaster relief, etc. All these applications involve spatially distributed, heterogeneous, unattended sensors, generating temporally dense observations. In other words, both relative and absolute location of sensors, and the time stamp on sensor observations determine the real world semantics of sensor data, that is, what sensor data imply about the state of the real world. The critical applications involving such sensor networks extend beyond sensing to control and actuation, and critical concerns associated with such applications will encompass reliability, robustness, usability, and privacy.

In 1999, Neil Gross expressed a vision of the future where sensors are ubiquitous and engrained in the fabric of our environment [Gross, 1999]: "*In the next century, planet earth will don an electronic skin. It will use the Internet as a scaffold to support and transmit its sensations. This skin is already being stitched together. It consists of millions of embedded electronic measuring devices: thermostats, pressure gauges, pollution detectors, cameras, microphones, glucose sensors, EKGs, electroencephalographs. These will probe and monitor cities and endangered species, the atmosphere, our ships, highways and fleets of trucks, our conversations, our bodies—even our dreams.*"

In 2008, Ramesh Jain described vast collections of event data as the Web's next evolution [Jain, 2008]: "*EventWeb organizes data in terms of events and experiences and allows natural access from users' perspectives. For each event, EventWeb collects and organizes audio, visual, tactile, and other data to provide people with an environment for experiencing the event from their perspective. EventWeb also easily reorganizes events to satisfy different viewpoints and naturally incorporates new data types—dynamic, temporal, and live.*" Realizing the EventWeb requires services for extraction and processing of spatial and temporal data and events, registries for storing event data, services for event notification and update, shared STT ontologies for normalization, and extensions to Semantic Web query languages to deal with temporal and spatial information natively [Sheth and Perry, 2008]. Increasingly a broad variety of devices are becoming part of cyberinfrastructure. The vision of Internet of Things/Web of Things (IoT/WoT) is to identify, describe, link, monitor, and effect physical objects and their environment, to create "ambient intelligence" that can assist or relieve people in carrying out everyday

---

[2]http://wiki.knoesis.org/index.php/SSW

tasks. Realization of this vision requires (i) techniques and technologies to represent and reason about the state of the objects and their interactions as sanctioned by their semantics and the needs of the end-user application, and (ii) sensing, networking, and communication infrastructure to access and effect the objects. For instance, the humidity of the soil and the weather forecast can be used to determine watering schedule for the crops and trigger water sprinklers. The contents of a refrigerator and the expiration dates of perishable articles can be monitored to alert the owner about the food inventory and its safety. SSW discussed above can serve as a necessary foundation for building IoT/WoT.

CHAPTER 7

Semantics for Social Data

The Social Web, one created by user-generated content, and the Semantic Web, a vision of a Web of machine-understandable documents and data, are fast approaching to embrace a *Semantic Social Web* (SSocW). On this SSocW, which some see as a key component of Web 3.0, principles of knowledge representation, ontologies, and document-level metadata will be used to organize and analyze social media content.

Popular Web 2.0 technologies such as tagging, and resources such as blogging and book-marking sites, review sites, social networking sites, image and video sharing sites, have made it very easy for people to consume, produce, and share information. The social Web of today includes not only user generated content (UGC) on Web 2.0, but also links to all types of Web resources, and implicitly people, connections between people, and the connections that people make through social networks and all the social, cultural, and behavioral richness of the humans that participate on these networks.

The Semantic Web approach to making data more useful and meaningful also applies to the social data. Like other forms of data, SSocW starts with labeling (marking up, tagging, or annotating) the social data. This is often achieved by using a model of a domain with explicit or implicit agreement among its developers and users, and takes the form of nomenclatures, dictionaries, taxonomies, community-created repositories and knowledge bases, folksonomies or ontologies. Unlike sensors data, user-generated content contain richness of natural language that express complex human thoughts including sentiments and emotions. It is also unique because of its informal nature, and in some cases, length limitations such as on microblogs and because of its creation on-the-go on mobile devices. Correspondingly, for references and agreements, we may have to use a variety of sources, such as Linguistic Inquiry and Word Count (LIWC[1]) word list or dictionary to get word categories or a sense of the word usage (e.g., the word 'cried' is part of four word categories: sadness, negative emotion, overall affect, and a past tense verb), UrbanDictionary[2] to understand region-specific slang usage (and which describes itself as a "veritable cornucopia of streetwise lingo, posted and defined by its readers"), and MusicBrainz[3] (a comprehensive community-maintained knowledge base of musical artists, genres, albums, and tracks) which represents global community created and maintained metadata or knowledge about all things music. So depending on the type of analysis one wishes to perform on a music-related social media post, either or all of these above references may be used.

[1]http://www.liwc.net/
[2]http://www.urbandictionary.com/
[3]http://musicbrainz.org/

The annotations use reference models to make documents and data machine-understandable as well as easier to integrate and analyze. Both machines and humans can exploit the data by utilizing the rich relationships between data formally expressed using annotations. With the help of ontologies, it is possible to support richer forms of modeling and use declarative rules to reason over annotated data. As discussed in earlier chapters, communities in varied domains such as life sciences, health care, finance, and music have begun to provide ontologies with associated knowledge or instance bases (i.e., populated ontologies) that richly describe their domain. Services that allow the use of populated ontologies for annotation and smarter applications that exploit annotations and rules are becoming increasingly common.

While the Social Media has been very successful in simplifying the process of content production, consumption, and sharing, it has not been sophisticated enough to allow users to add or preserve the semantics behind the content. So, when a user is writing about an object, say a "Wii Microphone," there is no way for him to refer to a unique agreed-upon identifier for that object. Consequently, when someone is looking for information about a "Wii Microphone," it has traditionally not been easy on the Web to bring everything we know about the object to one place. One of the goals of the Semantic Web is to bridge this content gap on the Web. On the one hand, the social context surrounding the UGC has opened several opportunities for enriching user interaction with content. On the other hand, this same social aspect to content production has introduced new challenges because of the content's informal and unconventional nature.

In this chapter, we discuss some of the challenges in annotating UGC, a first step toward the realization of the SSocW. Using examples from real-world UGC, we show how domain knowledge can effectively complement statistical natural language-processing techniques for metadata creation.

7.1   NATURE OF SOCIAL DATA

The volume and variety of user-generated content has shown steep increase with the ubiquity of high-speed networks, affordable mobile devices, and easy-to-use social software. UGC on social media has unique characteristics that set it apart from the traditional content in news or scientific articles. Due to social media's personal and interactive communication format, UGC is inherently informal and unmediated. Off-topic discussions are common, making it difficult to automatically identify context. Content is often fragmented, violating the rules of English grammar, especially those generated by the teen and tween demographic. Some UGC are also terse by nature, such as Twitter posts, leaving minimal cues to automatically identify the theme. In addition, they contain domain- and demographic-specific slang, abbreviations, and entity variations. This is further exacerbated by the variability (e.g., BP oil spill, oil #spill in #gulf) and the creativity (e.g., BPee, spill baby spill) of expression. All of these factors make the process of automatically identifying what a social media snippet is actually about much harder. Consequently, an important challenge for Web 3.0 applications is the creation of accurate annotations from UGC to common referenced models, to facilitate its semantic analysis.

Perhaps the most interesting phenomenon about such UGC is that it acts as a lens into the social perception of an event in any region, at any point in time. Citizen sensing [Sheth, 2009], or netizen's observations and views about the same event relayed from the same or different location, offer multiple, complementary viewpoints or storylines about an event. Furthermore, these viewpoints evolve over time, and influence regional neighborhoods. Consequently, in addition to what is being said about an event (theme), where (spatial) and when (temporal) it is said, are also critical and integral components to the meaningful analysis of such data. This makes social media inherently multidimensional in nature and taking these dimensions into account while processing, aggregating, connecting, and visualizing data will provide useful organization and consumption principles. *To improve scalability and quality of social perception gleaned from social data such as microblogs, it is necessary to perform fine-grained, real-time analysis of social data, and employ better data-intensive, contemporary language models to mirror its inherent dynamic and informal nature.*

The example depicted in Figure 7.1 shows metadata gathered from Twitter updates and Flickr images posted during the Mumbai attacks.[4] One can use it to extract spatial information about a resource (such as geo-coordinates from where a picture was taken or from where a message was posted) to determine the closest street address. From the image information in Figure 7.1, for example, we can identify the closest street address as 5 Hormusji Street, Colaba, Mumbai. When given to an "address to location" service, this information yields prominent locations near this address, including the Nariman House, Vasant Vihar, and the Income Tax Office. Next, by using temporal information from the image, we can get Twitter messages posted around the time it was taken; spatial information helps restrict the geography to just where these messages originated. The location information in conjunction with semantic models that describe a particular domain of interest (terrorism, in this context) let us connect tweets that describe the event to images found in Flickr. Such integration provides a richer description of the event and lets us create trails of various events.

Even though the quality of crowd-sourced information cannot always be guaranteed, because of its diversity and decentralization, it can provide trends and relationships based on aggregate statistics that may be more accurate and quicker to obtain compared to similar information from the experts, especially in emergency situations or when faced with accessibility restrictions. Humans are much better at contextualizing and discerning data, filtering them across multiple modalities, and encapsulating the essence.

7.2   ROLE OF SEMANTICS IN SOCIAL MEDIA

The role of ontologies and knowledge bases in creating annotations is growing in significance with the growth of the social Web and the diversity of social media content. Ontologies and background knowledge can act as common reference models and play a significant role in inferring semantics behind UGC, supplementing well-known statistical and natural language processing (NLP) techniques. For example, named entity identification and disambiguation [Nadeau and Sekine, 2007] will pose a significant challenge for search and content integration which can be addressed using

[4]http://wiki.knoesis.org/index.php/Citizen_Sensing

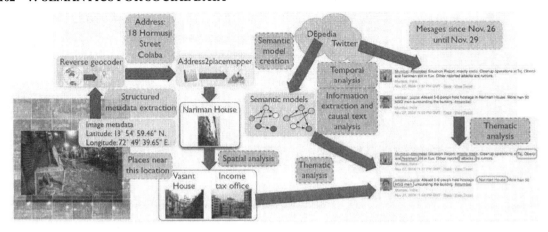

Figure 7.1: Semantic annotation of citizen-sensor data integrates raw information from citizen-sensors and leads to situational awareness [Sheth, 2009] (copyright © IEEE, with permission).

background knowledge more economically than statistical NLP techniques. Besides entity spotting, semantic techniques will enable normalization and linking of extracted concepts/entities, elimination of spam and off-topic discussions, and aggregation of sentiments. Social media spans multiple content types, people networks, and people–content interactions. Semantics can play a critical role to effectively organize and exploit this avalanche of information and build applications that enrich online user experience or provide business intelligence.

7.3   CREATION/APPLICATION OF SEMANTIC METADATA: MODELS AND ANNOTATIONS

We now discuss various practical uses of background knowledge and illustrate its exploitation in social/business intelligence application.[5]

7.3.1   DISAMBIGUATING ENTITY MENTIONS

Consider the following post on a music group's discussion board: "Lily I loved your cheryl tweedy do ... heart Amy." The post is referring to artist Lily Allen's music track 'Cheryl Tweedy.' The poster Amy also shares a first name with a popular artist 'Amy Winehouse.' Assuming that the end goal is to annotate artist and track/album mentions, the task here is to decide whether entities Lily, Cheryl Tweedy, and Amy in the post are of interest. In such cases of ambiguity, a knowledge base along with explicated relationships will provide context in addition to word distributions in a corpus. A domain model, such as MusicBrainz, for example, will state that "Cheryl Tweedy"

[5]http://www.slideshare.net/knoesis/citizen-sensor-data-mining-social-media-analytics-and-development-centric-web-applications-7361064

is a track by artist 'Lily Allen.' 'Amy Winehouse' and 'Lily Allen' are different artists from different genres—Pop and Jazz respectively. The lack of additional support for 'Amy' from the knowledge base in spite of capitalized first letters and the sentence parse assigning a noun tag (see Figure 7.2) could be taken into consideration before annotating the mention.

7.3.2   IDENTIFYING ENTITIES

In the post, "`Lils smile so rocks,`" the knowledge base tells us that "Smile" is a track by "Lily Allen" (with a high string similarity between "Lily" and "Lils") and is a possible entity of interest. This can be considered as a form of support toward "Smile" being a named entity of interest in spite of its verb (VBP), part of speech tag (see Figure 7.2b), and lack of first letter capitalization. Similarly, in the tweet, "`Steve says: All Zunes and OneCares must go, at prices permanently slashed!,`" one can conclude that "Steve" here is referring to "Steve Ballmer," Microsoft's CEO, given that a knowledge base, which serves to unravel the implicit context, mentions Zunes and OneCares as Microsoft products and Steve Ballmer as the company's CEO.

7.3.3   ROBUSTNESS WITH RESPECT TO OFF-TOPIC NOISE

Removing off-topic noise is important for understanding what the content is about. Consider the following post from a social network forum in which the user is talking about a project using "Sony Vegas Pro 8" but digresses to other topSheth2009words "Merrill Lynch," "food poisoning," and "eggs" are clearly off-topic in this context:

```
     I NEED HELP WITH SONY VEGAS PRO 8!! Ugh and i have a video project due
tomorrow for merrill lynch :( all i need to do is simple: Extract several
scenes from a clip, insert captions, transitions and thats it. really. omgg
i can't figure out anything!! help!! and i got food poisoning from eggs.
its not fun. Pleasssse, help? :(
```

In addition to association strengths between words (derived from a corpus), a knowledge base of computer software will readily tell us that none of the off-topic keywords are relevant to the discussion about "Sony Vegas Pro." The presence of off-topic noise especially affects the results of content-analysis applications when a strong monetary value is associated with the content [Nagarajan et al., 2009a]. User activity on social networking forums that contain explicit purchase intents are excellent contenders for monetization. Advertisements shown on this medium have high visibility and also higher chances of being clicked provided they are relevant to the user content. Figure 7.3 shows an example of the targeted nature of advertisements delivered before and after removing off-topic noise.

7.3.4   ANALYZING USER COMMENTS

A content-analysis system that mined music-artist popularity from user comments on MySpace artist pages was implemented [Grace et al., 2007]. The system contained (i) an artist and music annotator to spot artists, albums, tracks, and other music-related mentions (such as labels, tours,

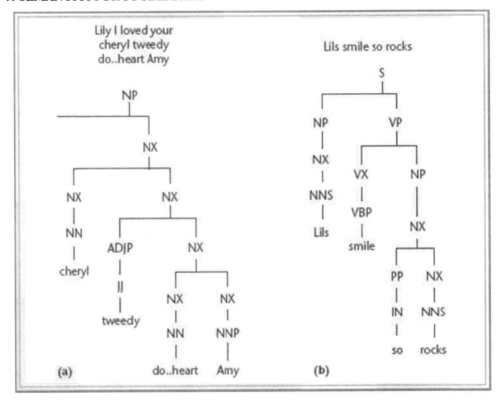

Figure 7.2: A syntactic parse of a user-generated comment from MySpace. (a) A singular proper noun tag assigned to the ambiguous entity "Amy." (b) A verb, non-third-person-singular present assigned to the word "smile." [Sheth and Nagarajan, 2009] (copyright © IEEE, with permission).

shows, and concerts) in user posts, and (ii) a sentiment annotator to detect sentiment expressions and measure their polarities.

MusicBrainz was used as a backend for the artist and music annotator. The annotator compared artist or track mentions in user comments against artist entries and associated track entries in the knowledge base to gain more context. In addition to this, the annotator used results of a syntactic parse of the comment and corpus statistics to annotate a track or artist mention. The sentiment annotator used a syntactic parse of comments to extract adjectives and verbs as potential sentiment expressions. It then consulted UrbanDictionary[6] to verify an expression's validity and ascertain polarity (positive or negative). For example, the slang expression "wicked" has the same sense as the expressions "cool," "awesome," "sweet," "sick," "amazing," "great," "bad," etc., deviating from, and in some cases in stark contrast with, their traditional meanings.

[6]UrbanDictionary.com

Figure 7.3: Contextual advertisements. The top half shows a user post and ads generated when content has off-topic keywords, and the bottom half shows ads after we eliminate off-topic keywords [Sheth and Nagarajan, 2009]. (copyright © IEEE, with permission).

For both annotators, the combination of techniques proved to be more useful than using techniques in isolation. Positive and negative sentiments for all artists were aggregated, and a ranked list of the top X artists ordered by the number of positive sentiment comments were generated (see Figure 7.4). By observing popularity trends over time and the patterns that stand out in the user activity of such online communities it was possible to forecast what was going to be popular tomorrow.

7.3.5   AGGREGATING ATTENTION METADATA

User-generated textual content such as reviews, posts, and discussions are only one example of attention metadata. Other examples include

- descriptions, tags, and user-placed anchor links;

- page views and access logs;

- star ratings and diggs; and

- images, audio, video, and other multimedia content.

Today, applications that aggregate user activity typically operate with only one type of attention metadata. They might aggregate topical blogs, visualize connections between people and the content produced within a network, or aggregate music listening. Aggregating all known attention metadata for an object is complicated because it involves multimodal information [Alba et al., 2008]. With the need to measure a population's pulse across all available information sources, this will continue to be an important area of investigation.

7.3.6   ANNOTATING AND REASONING WITH SOCIAL MEDIA

Annotating UGC with common reference models will undoubtedly improve applications tasked with presenting a holistic view of all information available to a user. Content-delivery applications such as Zemanta (`http://www.zemanta.com/`), for example, that match keywords to provide related information, can utilize related concepts in the knowledge base to suggest additional content. Perhaps the most interesting phenomenon on the social Web is that people are not only connected to each other by means of a social tie (friends on social networks or referrals on LinkedIn) but are also connected via a piece of information. A user can link to someone's blog post, for example, follow someone's tweet, respond to a posting, tweet with other users from the same location, and so on. In addition to context derived from the content, a corpus, or a domain knowledge base, UGC also comes with a social context that includes the network in which it was generated. For certain types of data, such as tweets sent from a cell phone, there is also a situational context, such as time and location, which becomes increasingly relevant to the analysis. Tapping this machine-accessible people–content network and its associated social and situational contexts empowers a new breed of personalized socially aware systems [Mika, 2007]. Imagine a scenario in which you are looking to get more information about a camera you heard described on the radio, but you do not remember the exact model number. However, you do remember the radio host mentioned his blog post, which discussed a review he had read on his favorite gadget discussion forum for the same product. On the social Semantic Web, where all UGC is annotated, an intelligent search program would be able to sift through all of the host's blog posts and all the annotated gadget forum posts, look for the same camera object, and return matching pages to you. Now, consider the following scenario in which an event-tracker system maintains a knowledge base of music events (including dates, times, and locations) along with artists and their work; it also continually tracks and annotates tweets related to the events. Now imagine a user tweet, "Hitting traffic jam. Looks like im missin lilys opening" from his iPhone (which also provides time and location information). Using situational context information and identifying "Lily" in the tweet, the system has enough support to associate this message with the "Lily Allen concert" event in its knowledge base. The application can now alert users who have signed up for the same event and share similar location coordinates with a "watch out for a traffic jam" message.

7.3.7   THE BBC SOUNDINDEX APPLICATION

The BBC SoundIndex [Gruhl et al., 2010] enables real-time analytics of music popularity using data from a variety of Social Networks. This application transforms Social Intelligence into Business Intelligence in the music domain. It required the use of background knowledge to overcome several

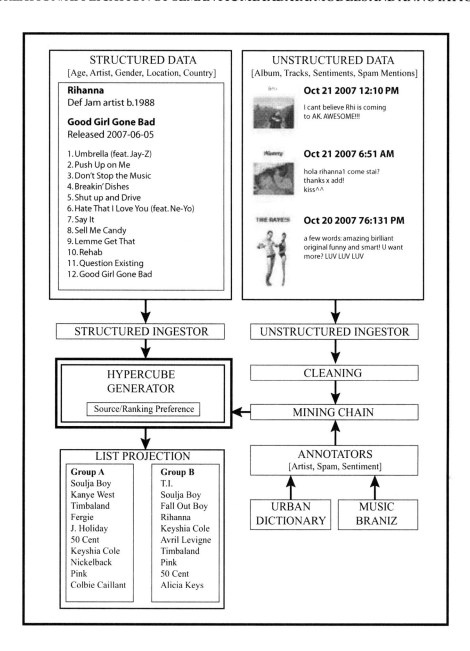

Figure 7.4: System architecture. The use of domain knowledge helps analyze user-generated content for the task of popularity mining [Sheth and Nagarajan, 2009] (copyright © IEEE, with permission).

challenges to tap into the wisdom of the crowds in near real-time, such as obtaining data from a wide set of sources (e.g., MySpace/Twitter, iTunes/Amazon, YouTube, LastFM) spanning different modalities (e.g., comments, sale figures, video views statistics, track listen statistics), developing adjudication techniques to harmonize inputs (using rank aggregation), performing deep analytics on challenging informal English snippets (with non-standard abbreviations, slang, and context-sensitive terms, violating grammar and spelling rules) to identify concepts and sentiments, dashboard-type visualization, etc. Identifying and disambiguating named entity mentions in text is difficult when there is insufficient context, or when entity references conflict with commonly used words such as "Up," "Yesterday," "Imagine," "Blow," "Love Story," etc. In order to overcome this problem, Gruhl et al. [2010] present an approach to gleaning real-world constraints from music-related text fragments that can be used to systematically pare down applicable domain models to reduce the entity spot set and thereby improve the precision of the spotter. Figure 7.5 shows the BBC SoundIndex Architecture to automate this process. For example, characteristics of an artist gleaned from the comments referring to birthday, gender, an album release, etc., can be used to restrict MusicBrainz RDF. A comment such as "Happy 25th B-DAY!" restricts the MusicBrainz RDF to only a small fraction of the artists in MusicBrainz who have this birth year. In the end, it was discovered that the near real-time information about the popularity of various artists, tracks, and genres of music generated by analyzing online discussions, music requests, and purchases, was far more reliable than the traditional metric involving record sales and radio plays used by Billboard.

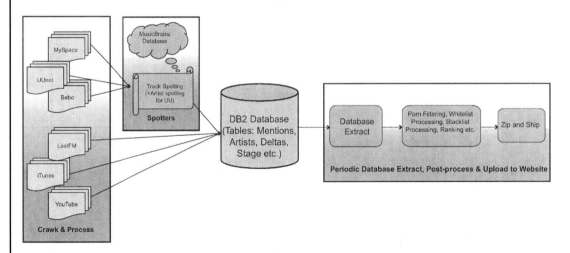

Figure 7.5: SoundIndex architecture. Data sources are ingested and transformed into structured data using the MusicBrainz RDF and data miners. The resulting structured data are stored in a database and periodically extracted to update the front end [Gruhl et al., 2010] (Copyright © Springer, with permission).

7.3.8   HARNESSING TWITTER: TWITRIS AND TWARQL APPLICATIONS

As of March 21, 2012 (Twitter's sixth birthday), its 140+ million users send out over 340 million tweets a day. In the recent years, we have seen Twitter as a significant platform for disseminating information and understanding the evolution of significant events of local and global importance. Global events where Twitter played pivotal roles include the Mumbai terrorist attack, the Iran elections, the Haiti earthquake, and US healthcare debate. Equally important are events of local and regional importance such as the Gilroy garlic festival and the Ohio State Fair that reflect traditional values of the culture. While Twitter has captured the imagination of the developed world, there is an equally impressive revolution going on in the developing world and emerging regions. Ushahidi.org and a number of other platforms such as eMoksha.org, Kiirti.org, and SMSGupShup.com cater to a much larger segment of 4.1 billion mobile phone (that are not smartphones) users to share UGC using SMS. The range of applications of this include emergency monitoring and management (e.g., pakreport.org), social activism (e.g., coalition against corruption), citizen awareness and engagement for strengthening democracies, education, rural development, and public health. Many of the interactions over these platforms are centered on events and activities. In some events such as the Haiti earthquake, both Twitter and SMS-based UGC were extensively used.

While current technologies have enabled easy access and sharing of social media content, there is a serious need to aggregate relevant social media and Web content, and analyze them to understand events as they unfold. For example, the following are some interesting questions that could have been asked during recent events for improving situational awareness:

> During the Mumbai terrorist attack, what were the main topics (key phrases) discussed in the tweets originating from Mumbai during each of the three days of carnage?

> During the Haiti earthquakes or recent Pakistan floods, what were the primary immediate requirements in rescue situations, and where were the possible locations from which supplies that match requirements offered?

> During recent Malaria outbreak in Rampir No Tekra (Gujarat's largest slum near Gandhi's Sabarmati Ashram), identify early SMSs and/or tweets that mentioned water logging, and plot them by time and location.

Current keyword-based search or other mechanisms (e.g., hashtags in tweets) are simply too inadequate for such purposes.

Twitris[7] is a tool that extracts social signals for sensemaking (that is, understanding connections between people, places, and events), which uses the spatio-temporal-thematic metadata extracted from the observations to summarize the semantic content, to create a mashup for visualizing the spatio-temporal-thematic aspects, and to provide a foundation for exploring other news and information sources [Nagarajan et al., 2009b]. Twitris starts with a static set of tweets about an event, partitions it into subsets based on spatio-temporal information associated with the tweets and the

---

[7]http://twitris.knoesis.org

nature of the event, and processes each spatio-temporal slice. Event descriptors, which summarize a spatio-temporal slice of tweets, are in the form of statistically significant N-grams that have been extracted from the tweets. Furthermore, while a corpus of tweets can go a long way in determining event descriptors, the variability and creativity of expression makes the statistics solely drawn from a corpus of tweets inadequate to yield quality event descriptors. Twitris (see Figure 7.5): (1) captures semantics from three contexts: internal context (context obtained by analyzing directly mentioned content, annotated entities, and related posts based on event descriptors), external context (obtained from external sources by semantically following the theme of the current post), and mined internal context (entity-relationship, sentiment analysis); (2) uses deep semantics, especially employing automatically created domain models [Sheth et al., 2010], to understand the meaning of standard event descriptors; (3) uses shallow semantics (semantically annotated entities) for knowledge discovery and representation, and (4) performs semantic integration of multiple external Web resources (news, articles, images, and videos) utilizing the semantic similarity between contexts.

In other words, current Twitris has been enhanced to perform semantics-empowered analysis of social media content with an aim to capture (1) semantics (i.e., meaning and understanding) along spatial, temporal, thematic dimensions, (2) user intentions and sentiments, and (3) networking behavior (user interaction patterns and features such as information diffusion, influence, and centrality). Semantic Web technologies enable its core integration, analysis, and data/knowledge sharing abilities. The system is currently being used for a number of *People-Content-Network-Sentiment* (PCNS) study experiments and is being extended to integrate with SMS and other Web data used by widely deployed open source projects. These include applications used by non-governmental organizations (NGOs) in developing countries for crisis management (in particular, Ushahidi.org, eMoksha.org, and Kiirti.org). Twitris is being adapted to a cloud platform for scalability.

Twarql focuses on querying, personalization, and analysis of real-time Twitter stream [Mendes et al., 2010]. It starts with support for annotations of Twitter stream. It supports encoding information from microblogs as Linked Open Data in order to enable their flexible analysis. Instead of requiring the use of keywords or custom software for filtering information, Twarql leverages a full-fledged query language (SPARQL) that is much more expressive than keywords. Specifically, SPARQL makes extensive use of existing ontologies and Semantic Web technologies. The approach encompasses the following steps: (1) extract content (entity mentions, hashtags, and URLs) from microblogs; (2) encode content in a structured format (RDF) using shared vocabularies (FOAF, SIOC, MOAT, etc.); (3) enable structured querying of microblogs (using SPARQL); (4) enable subscription to a stream of microblogs that match a given query (Concept Feeds); and (5) enable scalable real-time delivery of streaming data (SparqlPuSH). Twarql is available at `http://twarql.sf.net` as open source and can be easily extended and deployed to enable Twitter monitoring systems that can be used in various contexts: brand tracking, disaster relief management, stock exchange monitoring, etc.

By using agreed-upon semantic formats to describe people, content objects, and the connections that bind them all together, social media sites can interoperate by appealing to common

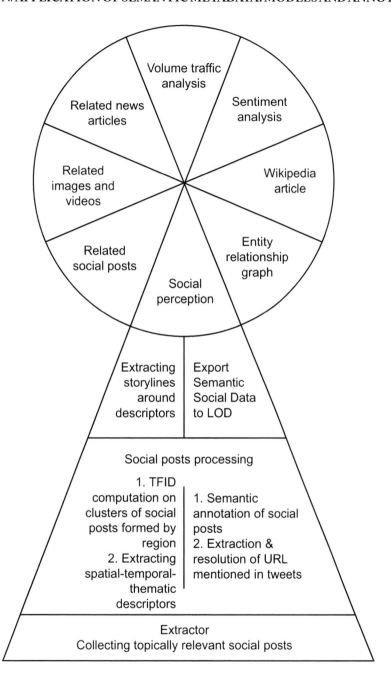

Figure 7.6: Twitris+ functional overview.

semantics.[8] In addition to the role that semantic background knowledge plays in identification, disambiguation, and aggregation of information as discussed above, there are several different efforts to ease creation, standardization, and machine comprehension of social data using ontologies to realize SSocW. Some prominent examples of these efforts include:

- FOAF (Friend of a Friend): An ontology for describing people and their relationships. (`http://foaf-project.org/`).

- SIOC (Semantically-Interlinked Online Communities): To fully describe content and structure of social websites, and facilitate creation and integration of online communities. (`http://sioc-project.org/`).

- SCOT (Social Semantic Cloud of Tags): To describe tag clouds for reuse and portability. (`http://www.scot-project.org/`).

- MOAT (Meaning of a Tag): A collaborative approach to share meanings in a community by providing a way for users to define meaning(s) of their tag(s) using URIs of Semantic Web resources. (`http://moat-project.org/`).

- SKOS (Simple Knowledge Organization System): To support the use of knowledge organization systems (KOS) such as thesauri, classification schemes, subject heading systems, and taxonomies within the framework of the Semantic Web. (`http://www.w3.org/2004/02/skos/`).

- SMOB (Semantic microblogging): To enable semantic tagging of microblogs, and their decentralized and distributed publishing.

- Semantic Wikis: To capture information about a page in a formal language, letting machines process and reason with it. (`http://www.semwiki.org/`).

- Semantic MediaWiki: An extension of MediaWiki, allowing users to add structured information to pages. (`http://semantic-mediawiki.org/`).

- OGP (Open Graph Protocol): To enable annotating a Web page to become a rich object in the social graph. Facebook's social graph represents people and the connections (e.g., like, friend, listen, and cook) they have to everything they care about (`http://ogp.me/`).

- GKG (Google's Knowledge Graph): To enrich query responses by providing structured information about the subject of a query besides a list of links. Google's Knowledge graph, which harnesses Freebase (`http://www.freebase.com/`), represents information about the real-world objects and their relationships.

---

[8]`http://www.slideshare.net/Cloud/the-social-semantic-web`

- Metadata Reference Link (MREF): To enrich hyperlinks with semantic information. Semantic metadata approach embodied in OGP, GKG, and semantic microblogging (SMOB) is similar to Sheth's Metadata Reference Link (MREF) proposed in 1996 that associates metadata with hypertext that links documents on the Web.

- Scheme.org: A collection of schemas, i.e., HTML tags constituting shared vocabulary, that webmasters can use to markup their pages in microdata format for indexing by major search engines including Bing, Google, and Yahoo! and Yandex. This also provides seemless integration of structured data. (`http://schema.org/`).

Today, communities in varied domains such as life sciences, healthcare, finance, and music have begun to provide ontologies with associated knowledge or instance bases to richly describe their domains. Services that allow the use of populated ontologies for annotation, and applications that can exploit annotations and rules, are becoming increasingly common [Sheth et al., 2002]. To the extent that social media content deals with these domains, semantic technologies will improve the quality of content, and eventually, user satisfaction. We see great potential for integration of social Web and the Semantic Web, where objects are treated as first-class citizens, making it easier to search, integrate, and exploit the information surrounding them. Although there are important content-related challenges to be met, applications using the semantic infrastructure will significantly enhance the business potential behind UGC as well as enrich user experience associated with social media.

CHAPTER 8

Semantics for Cloud Computing

Cloud computing holds unlimited promise for providing a utility style, pay-as-you-go, elastic computing paradigm. However, the cloud computing landscape is still evolving and there is a multitude of challenges to be overcome, to foster its wide spread adoption. At the forefront of these challenges is the issue of interoperability caused by heterogeneity and vendor lock-ins, as each vendor introduces its own framework and services. Although there are many efforts underway to standardize important technical aspects of computing clouds, notably from NIST, consolidation and standardization are still far from being realized. In this chapter, we discuss how a little-bit of semantics can help address key interoperability and portability issues faced by cloud computing today [Sheth and Ranabahu, 2010a,b].

8.1   NATURE OF CLOUD SERVICES

Figure 8.1 shows three main flavors of clouds as outlined by NIST (http://csrc.nist.gov/groups/SNS/cloud-computing/). The infrastructure-as-a-service (IaaS) cloud has the largest gap (heaviest workload/least automation) in terms of deploying an application and managing it in the cloud. This workload is substantially reduced (at the expense of flexibility and portability) when using a platform-as-a-service (PaaS) or a software-as-a-service (SaaS). Given the diverse environment, a cloud service consumer faces multiple challenges in selecting a cloud and working with it:

1. Depending on the requirements of the application, legal issues, and possible other considerations, the consumer has to *select* which cloud to use. Each cloud vendor exposes these details in different formats and at different levels of granularity.

2. The consumer then needs to acquire knowledge of the technical aspects (service interface, scaling configuration, etc.) and the workflow of the particular cloud provider. All these details are vendor specific.

3. Then the consumer develops an application or customizes the vendor-provided multi-tenant application to fulfill its requirements. This requires a variety of vendor-specific technical details to be sorted out including the choice of programming language and limitations in the application runtime.

4. Once the application is deployed, if the need arises to change the service provider (a requirement that arises surprisingly often), there are at least two major considerations.

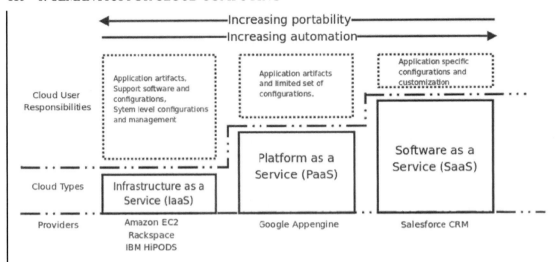

Figure 8.1: Cloud Landscape [Sheth and Ranabahu, 2010a] (copyright © IEEE, with permission).

(a) The code of the application may need to be rewritten or modified to suit the new provider's environment. For some clouds (such as IaaS) this is minimal but platform and software clouds require more effort in porting the code.

(b) The data that have been collected for the application may need to be transformed. Data constitute the most important asset the application generates over time and is essential for its continued functioning. These data transformations may even need to carry across different data models. Unfortunately, the current industry practice is to address such data transformations on a case-by-case basis.

Two types of heterogeneities commonly occur in practice: within single silo (or vertical) and across silo (or horizontal).

1. Vertical heterogeneity may be addressed using middleware to homogenize the API and sometimes by enforcing standardization. For example, Open Virtualization Format (OVF) (http://www.dmtf.org/vman/) is an emerging standard that allows the migration of virtual machine snapshots across IaaS clouds, facilitating vertical interoperability.

2. Horizontal heterogeneity is fundamentally harder to overcome. Each silo provides different levels of abstractions and services. A high-level modeling effort especially pays off when one needs to move application and code across different types of clouds.

Surprisingly many small and medium businesses make horizontal transitions. Platform clouds (PaaS) offer faster setup for applications and many take advantage of the free hosting opportunities of some of the platform cloud providers (e.g., Google AppEngine). When the application grows in scope and criticality however, an IaaS Cloud may prove to be cheaper, more flexible, and more reliable, prompting a transition.

8.2   ROLE OF SEMANTIC MODELING IN CLOUD COMPUTING

In order to overcome these challenges, we outline the role of semantic modeling in the cloud space, which is applicable to both vertical and horizontal interoperability. The key to addressing interoperability lies in the fact that many of the core data and services causing these heterogeneities to follow the same semantic concepts. For example, almost all the IaaS clouds follow conceptually similar workflows when allocating resources, although the actual service implementations and tools differ significantly. Similarly, the modeling space for a PaaS is a subset of the modeling space for IaaS, from a semantic perspective.

In practice, detailed semantic models have found relevance in new applications and technologies to provide improved functionality (e.g., biomedical ontologies cataloged at the National Center for Biomedical ontologies), especially, to make inferences and gain new knowledge, in spite of large upfront investments. These capabilities are being complemented by the ability to more rapidly create up-to-date domain models, often by mining crowd knowledge represented, for example, in Wikipedia [Thomas et al., 2008] or shared data exemplified by the Linked Object Data cloud.

We suggest a three-dimensional *slicing* of the modeling requirements along the dimensions of type, level of abstraction, and software lifecycle state.

1. The *type of semantics* that is useful for portability and interoperability in cloud computing are similar to those for Web services [Sivashanmugam et al., 2003]. This is natural since the primary means of interacting with a cloud environment is through Web services. The four types—data, logic/process, non-functional, and system—are based on the different semantic aspects a model would need to cover.

2. The *level of abstraction* is an indicator of the granularity and specificity of the modeling. Although ontological modeling is favored at a higher level, detailed and concrete syntactic representations are preferred by the developers. These representations of different granularities may need to be related/reconciled in many occasions via explicit annotations (such as using SAWSDL.[1])

3. *Software life cycle state* also plays an important role in determining the modeling requirement. For example, some non-functional and system requirements may not be modeled at the development phase but only taken into account during deployment. Each of these life cycle stages are handled by different teams, and this separation is important for each of these parties to *not step on each other's toes*.

---

[1]http://www.w3.org/TR/sawsdl/

Some of the existing Cloud models, such as the three OWL-based modeling languages, ECML, EDML, and ECML [Charlton, 2009], published by Elastra Inc., fall under the non-functional/system/ontology space as depicted in Figure 8.2.

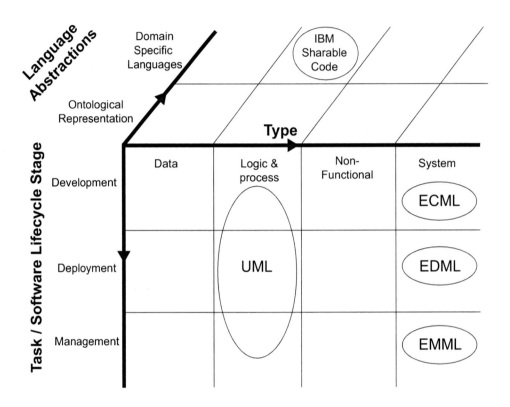

Figure 8.2: A multi-dimensional slicing of the modeling space for Cloud computing [Sheth and Ranabahu, 2010b].

This design space also shows that some aspects have received little or no attention at all. For example, there is no comprehensive higher-level modeling in the data and functional spaces. Lessons learned during the large-scale ontological modeling efforts in semantic Web and semantic Web services, biology, and many other domains are readily applicable here and would be beneficial in addressing challenges in the cloud space.

We introduce four types of semantics for an application, inspired by the four types of semantics for a service in Chapter 5. This partitioning is necessary to model the different concerns at a high level in a platform agnostic manner. The term *application* is used to mean a software program designed to help the user to perform singular or multiple related specific tasks. The identified types of semantics are shown in Figure 8.3 and discussed below:

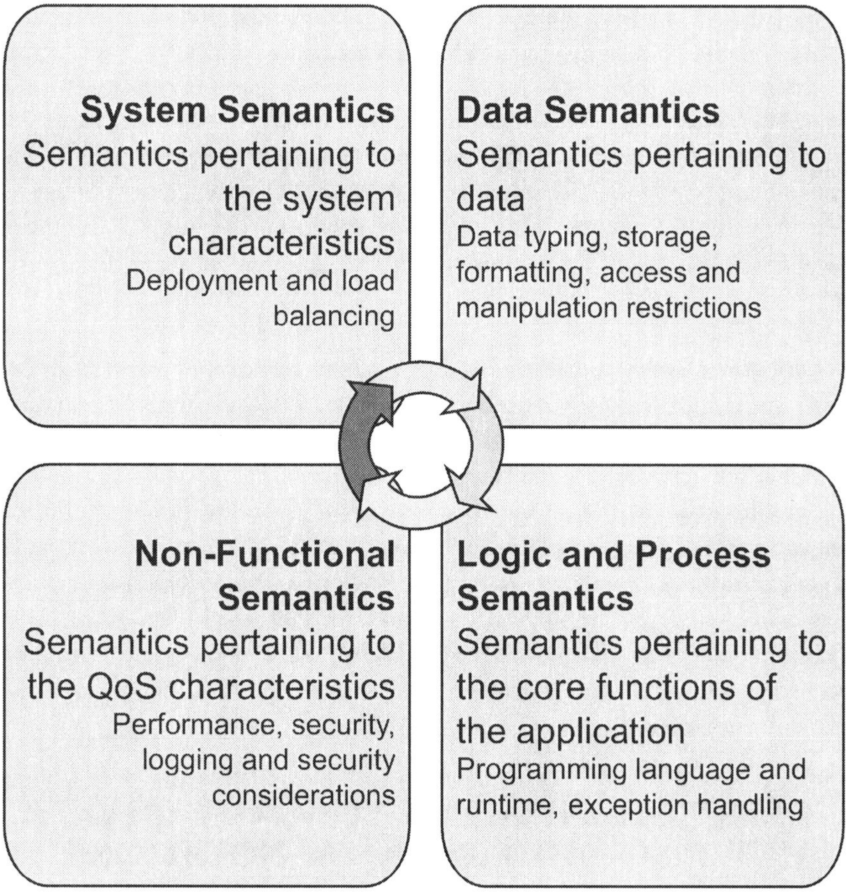

System Semantics
Semantics pertaining to the system characteristics
Deployment and load balancing

Data Semantics
Semantics pertaining to data
Data typing, storage, formatting, access and manipulation restrictions

Non-Functional Semantics
Semantics pertaining to the QoS characteristics
Performance, security, logging and security considerations

Logic and Process Semantics
Semantics pertaining to the core functions of the application
Programming language and runtime, exception handling

Figure 8.3: The four types of semantics [Ranabahu, 2012].

Data Semantics: Data semantics address the data aspects of an application. This includes definitions of data structures, relationships across multiple data structures, as well as restrictions on the access of some of the data items. A crucial issue developers face today is the difficulty to port data horizontally across clouds due to lack of platform agnostic data model. For example, moving data from a schema-less data store (such as Google BigTable [Chang et al., 2008]) to a schema-driven data store such as a relational database presents a significant challenge. Semantic modeling of data to provide a platform independent data representation would be a major advantage in the cloud space.

Logic and process semantics: These pertain to the core functionality (commonly referred to as the business logic) of an application. Unlike in a service, the functional and execution semantics are tightly tied together for an application. For example, behavior of a service during an exception may be handled externally although exceptions are an integral part of the core functionality of an application and seldom designed separately. Lightweight semantics has special applicability here.

Non-functional semantics: While these are not part of the core functions, an application nevertheless requires them to be defined. Examples of non-functional semantics include information about quality of service (QoS), access control, and logging, which may require libraries or internal code changes. W.r.t. logging, an application internally implements the points of logging but the users get to control the granularity of the entries such as INFO (informational content) vs. ERROR (only errors).

System semantics: System semantics govern the system-related concerns of an application. Relevant considerations include deployment descriptions and dependency management. These considerations are neither relevant to the business logic nor to the non-functional considerations but become important when the application starts running on a system. For example, computing clouds expose their operations via Web Services but these service interfaces are different from vendor to vendor. The semantics of the operations however are very similar. Metadata added via annotations pointing to generic operational models would play a key role in consolidating these APIs and enable interoperability among the heterogeneous cloud environments. In fact, semantic technologies are already being used in this space commercially. Elastra Inc. uses three ontologies (semantic models) to describe the configuration, deployment, and management details for an application deployed to an Infrastructure Cloud.

8.3   CREATION AND APPLICATION OF SEMANTIC METADATA: MODELS AND ANNOTATIONS

We now discuss how to associate semantics to various aspects of a program that runs in the cloud.

8.3.1   SEMANTICS FOR LOGICAL AND PROCESS PORTABILITY

To improve cloud interoperability, semantic models can be used to define logical and process aspects of applications in a target-platform agnostic form. However, converting a high-level model directly to executable artifacts ends up *polluting* both representations. So intermediate representations are important to provide gradual conversion from the higher-level models to lower-level, executable representations.

Traditional *model-driven development* uses UML to capture application functionality at a high level and generate application skeleton from it, abstracting away *low-level* details deliberately. Unfortunately, UML-driven object-oriented development processes depend heavily on advanced tools (e.g., Rational Rose from IBM) limiting its applicability. A viable alternative to this approach is the use of embedded Domain Specific Languages (DSL), based on scripting languages such as Ruby and Python, to define "executable" *lightweight model*. *Lightweight* here signifies that these models do not use rich knowledge representation languages, and as a result, have limited reasoning capabilities.

Cirrocumulus,[2] an early project focused on cloud interoperability, uses DSLs as a key enabler that can bridge the gap between executable artifacts and high-level semantic models. A DSL, although domain specific, is better capable of specifying semantic descriptions.

A *best-of-both-worlds* approach that allows convenience of lightweight models along with a support for high-level operations when required is to use *annotations* linking the models. Figure 8.4 shows an annotation referring to an ontology from a fictitious DSL script for configuration. In general, the annotation links relevant components between different levels of specification.

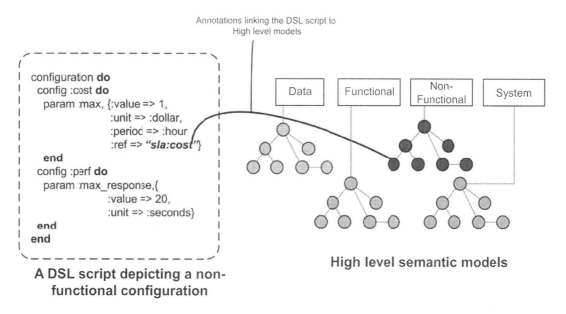

Figure 8.4: Annotating a DSL script (on left) with high-level semantic model (on right) (Functional semantics abbreviates logical and process semantics). [Sheth and Ranabahu, 2010b] (copyright © IEEE, with permission)

8.3.2   SEMANTICS FOR DATA MODELING

Another opportunity for semantic models for clouds lies in RDF data modeling to overcome data lock-in, i.e., the inability to port data horizontally. Many vendors use schema-less, distributed data stores with relaxed consistency models to provide high availability and elasticity. Unfortunately, this makes it hard for existing data driven applications to port data to a traditional, relational database, without substantial redesign on a case-by-case basis.

[2]http://knoesis.org/research/srl/projects/cirrocumulus/

Modeling data in RDF can support *generation of* different target representations, and in some cases, even code for data access layer of the application. Furthermore, it is possible to transform between various representations using the lifting-lowering mechanism, along the lines of SAWSDL [Nagarajan et al., 2006].

Lightweight modeling in terms of DSLs is also applicable in this space. For example, XML Schema definitions can be input to code generators to obtain platform specific data definitions.

8.3.3 SEMANTICS FOR SERVICE ENRICHMENT

Clouds normally provide Web services to manipulate resources, enabling programmatic management of its resources from within the same cloud. These capabilities have revolutionized how applications are deployed and managed. For example, well-defined services can be composed or *'mashed up'* to facilitate elaborate workflows.

Service definitions are usually syntactic, but recently researchers have focused on embedding rich semantic, machine-processable metadata into formal service descriptions. For example, SAWSDL standardizes semantic annotations in WSDL service descriptions. Similarly, annotation of HTML descriptions is gaining momentum because popular search engines use metadata to display search results in customized formats. For example, Yahoo! SearchMonkey and Google Rich Snippets are two such schemes that are driven by microformats. In general, annotations can be *structured* based on a controlled vocabulary or taxonomy or a full-fledged ontology. For example, the popular hCalendar microformat is based on structure and is part of the movement called "*lower case semantic web*" that emphasizes focus on lightweight models.

Embedding rich semantic metadata in cloud service descriptions have benefits that go beyond customized search capabilities as discussed below.

1. Many cloud service providers adopt REST style Web services that do not advocate a formal service description. These services are described using HTML pages. WSDL 2.0 explicitly included support to formally describe RESTful services but it has not seen quick adoption. Alternative approaches such as SA-REST [Sheth et al., 2007], a generic annotation scheme designed by following microformat design principles, are becoming more applicable in this space. These annotations enable seamless and flexible integration of formalizations into RESTful service descriptions opening the door to many exciting avenues such as faceted search to identify relevant reusable services and semi-automated service compositions.

2. The cloud space is still evolving and attaching formalizations via annotations is compatible with this trend. This is especially attractive to vendors who are not willing to invest heavily in interim standards.

3. The formalizations not only apply to the service descriptions but also to many other aspects such as Service Level Agreements (SLA) and software licenses. Annotations can be used to embed formalizations even for these documents facilitating more automation in the cloud space. For example, Web Service Level Agreements (WSLA) specification (`http://www.`

`research.ibm.com/wsla/`) provides a means of formalizing the SLAs though they are time consuming to create and maintain.

Figure 8.5 illustrates the use of SA-REST annotations on the Amazon EC2 SLA document and how a capable processor would be able to utilize these annotations to extract a WSLA equivalent of the human readable SLA.

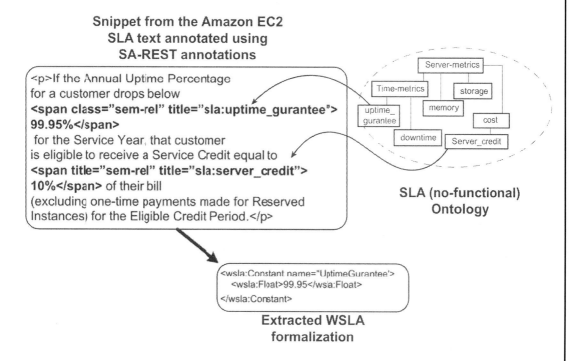

Figure 8.5: Embedding machine-processable metadata and extracting formal definitions. [Sheth and Ranabahu, 2010b] (copyright © IEEE, with permission)

8.4   EXAMPLES OF APPLICATIONS

We discuss two deployed cloud applications that illustrate the use of Domain Specific Language for specifying the semantics.

Cloud-mobile hybrid application: This application implements the back-end (data storage, partial business logic) in a cloud environment but has a mobile device based front-end (user interface). Mobicloud DSL, based on Model-View-Controller (MVC) design pattern, has been developed to address portability issues both at the front-end and at the back-end [Ranabahu et al., 2011b].

Currently, MobiCloud[3] tools are capable of producing Android and Blackberry applications as front-ends and Google App Engine (GAE) and Amazon EC2 applications as back-ends [Ranabahu et al., 2011b]. This approach requires us to provide translations of the order of sum of the number of mobile platforms and the number of cloud platforms (as opposed to their product). Even though DSLs seem to embody constructs that are the least common denominator of the available platforms, they can be extended to incorporate platform specific constructs.

Nuclear Magnetic Resonance-based Metabolomics Data Analysis: We have developed a set of fundamental operators for nuclear magnetic resonance (NMR) based metabolomics [Manjunatha et al., 2011]. The operators (such as normalization, quantification, scaling, and transformation) are implementation independent, and can be used to precisely describe the processing and analysis steps. They also facilitate inter-lab communication and can be adapted for use of the use of the metabolomics community. A DSL approach can be used to implement them because the DSL is simple and convenient for a domain scientist to use, and easy to translate to different cloud platforms.

To summarize, the cloud space presents many opportunities for researchers and a plethora of applications to utilize semantic modeling capability. Semantic models provide good solutions for interoperability and data portability problems faced by the cloud community. However, learning from the past, we advocate a multi-level modeling strategy in order to provide smooth transitions into different levels of granularity. DSLs can play an important role in the cloud space to provide lightweight modeling in an appealing manner to the software engineering community.

---

[3]http://mobicloud.knoesis.org/

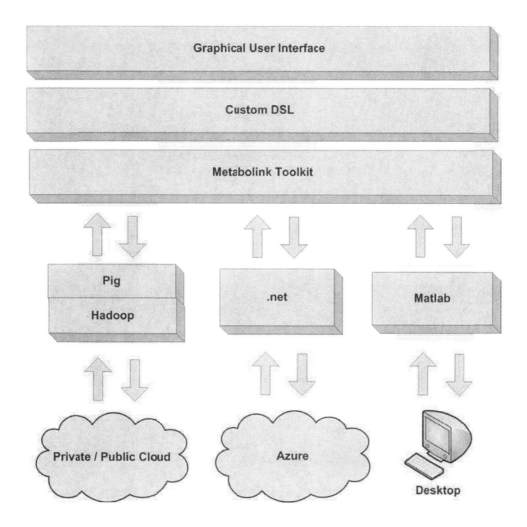

Figure 8.6: Layered Architecture for implementing DSL on Cloud [Manjunatha et al., 2011].

CHAPTER 9

Semantics for Advanced Applications

So far, we have discussed the role of semantics and semantic web technologies to bridge syntactic and structural heterogeneity for data integration and interoperation, to facilitate data disambiguation and interpretation, and to enable abstraction and search by reconciling semantic heterogeneity. In this chapter, we discuss more advanced situational awareness applications enabled by integrated use of mobile sensors, wireless connectivity, and/or sensor and social data. We also motivate novel techniques required to cater to their needs of dynamic background knowledge, harnessing LOD and crowd-sourced resources (such as Wikipedia). Ultimately, semantic techniques and technologies can facilitate realization of the Web of Things where everyday devices and objects (with embedded computers) are fully integrated into the Web, permitting their access, monitoring, and control. This will then be a stepping stone to the realization of the vision of Computing for Human Experience [Sheth, 2010] where semantics will integrate devices, data, analysis, and knowledge at physical, cyber, and social levels to assist and enhance all forms of human activities in a highly natural way.

9.1 ROBUST INTEGRATION OF SENSORS DATA: RECONCILING SEMANTIC HETEROGENEITY

In most real-world environments, there are many different types of sensors observing a situation. Figure 9.1 shows an example in the military context. The machine sensors can be as diverse as satellites, cameras, and GPS sensors, to weather station sensors providing temperature, wind speed, and precipitation measurements. Social sensors (a.k.a. citizen sensors) can provide situational information using smart phones (to deliver text messages via SMS) and via social networking sites (e.g., Twitter, Facebook). Machine sensors are objective and provide quantitative observational values by measuring low-level phenomenon; they are persistent and precise to a degree that cannot be matched by a human observer. On the contrary, social sensors are subjective and capable of providing a qualitative comprehensive interpretation of a situation very quickly and succinctly. Specifically, similar machine-sensed values can have different real-world interpretations from the eye of an observer or a decision maker. For example, a slow moving traffic registered by a traffic flow sensor can be explained by anything from rush hour traffic on a weekday, to that prevailing before and after a rock concert near its arena, to that caused by a car accident or due to icy road conditions. In general, the real-world event that explains the machine sensed observation can be determined systematically by checking if the prevailing situation can be accounted for by a typical traffic pattern based on the spatio-temporal context, or by an occurrence of a planned event, or in exceptional but critical cases, by gleaning cause from socially sensed observations sent via tweets from mobile devices. In essence, machine sensors and social sensors can provide complementary and corroborative information. They can also enable disambiguation/conflict resolution. Thus, semantic integration of heterogeneous sensors using stratified background knowledge in the form of multiple ontologies (see Table 9.1) and hybrid abductive/deductive reasoning infrastructure can improve the quality of situational awareness by enhancing completeness and dependability. Abductive reasoning that underlies explanation generation can enable systematic interpretation of sensor data, and deductive reasoning that underlies prediction can enable the narrowing down of viable explanations. Ultimately, hybrid reasoning will be essential for proactively seeking and integrating heterogeneous sensor data to provide semantic perception—situation awareness and actionable intelligence enhanced by ontologies and/or background knowledge—to the decision makers. Table 9.1 shows the application of multiple ontologies for describing different sensors and sensor observations, and for information along different dimensions.

Table 9.1: Use of multiple ontologies in different contexts and for different purposes

	Sensor/Observation Ontology	Spatial Ontology	Temporal Ontology	Domain Ontology
Fixed machine sensor	Capabilities of sensor	Location of sensor	Time when sensor is active	Type of qualities that can be observed
Mobile machine sensor	Capabilities of sensor	Path of sensor	Time when sensor is active	Type of qualities that can be observed
Fixed machine observation	Detecting sensor	Location of observation	Time of observation	Type of quality observed
Mobile machine observation	Detecting sensor	Location of observation	Time of observation	Type of quality observed
Human observation	Detecting sensor	Location of observation	Time of observation	Type of quality observed

Machine sensing is prone to vagaries of environmental effects and malicious attacks, while social sensing (a.k.a. citizen sensing) is prone to cognitive bias, rumors, misunderstandings, and factual inaccuracies, accidentally by uninformed public or intentionally by miscreants. In order to improve trustworthiness of data provided by a sensor network, and to enable detection of anomaly, it is important to be able to cross check data provided by different sensors of a sensor network. For densely populated homogeneous sensor networks, one can expect and exploit spatio-temporal coherence in sensor data generated by sensors in spatio-temporal proximity. As such, statistical methods may be brought to bear to ascertain their consistency. On the other hand, such syntactic approaches are inadequate when dealing with heterogeneous sensor networks that contain sensors measuring

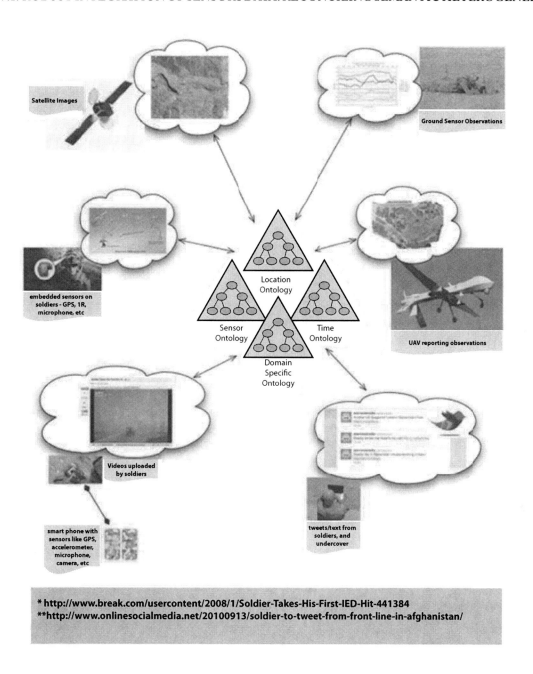

* http://www.break.com/usercontent/2008/1/Soldier-Takes-His-First-IED-Hit-441384
**http://www.onlinesocialmedia.net/20100913/soldier-to-tweet-from-front-line-in-afghanistan/

Figure 9.1: Integration of heterogeneous sensor data in military context.

different phenomenon (even when housed in the same sensor station), but where different sensor stations are relatively far apart. In such cases, domain models capturing semantic correlation among sensor data are necessary to reconcile semantic heterogeneity [Halevy, 2005, Henson et al., 2011, 2012a]. (For example, the color of the flame of a burning object and its temperature are correlated; values from co-located magnetometers, accelerometers, gyroscopes, and GPS are correlated.) Furthermore, anomaly detection in thinly populated sensor networks can require background knowledge specifying normalcy as a function of spatio-temporal coordinates. This issue is further complicated by the fact that "unexpected" sensor data may in fact represent an abnormal situation. That is, it may be impossible to distinguish an abnormal situation from a sensor fault purely on the basis of observational data (for example, freezing temperature in May vs. stuck-at-zero fault). In order to deal with this situation, we need to construct sensor fault models. Analogously, in the context of anomalous social data, we need to distinguish between occurrences of an abnormal event from utterances of uninformed public or malicious elements. We need to develop robust cause-effect models taking into account normalcy, faults, context, and intentions to distinguish data from compromised sensors (resp. malicious agent), legitimate data signaling abnormal situation (resp. unlikely event), and erroneous data from faulty sensors (resp. uninformed public). Given that it can be difficult to verbalize normalcy data and implicit constraints, it needs to be learned from training data.

Wireless sensor network nodes normally offload their sensed data, periodically or triggered by an event, to a data sink that is continuously connected to the Internet. In contrast, unattended wireless sensor network nodes are relatively sporadically polled by a mobile data sink, requiring extra power, storage, and security measures to keep the data intact. The latter nodes, which are commonly deployed in areas such as battle fields and border crossings, are more prone to compromise, due to illegal data readouts and tampering. To reduce power requirements and to avoid promiscuous readouts, sensors and RFID technologies are being combined to facilitate passive communication using RFID reader's power and to improve security with reads enabled only in an appropriately sensed semantic (spatio-temporal-thematic) context.

Recently, sensors and mobile computing devices are increasingly being used to monitor and manage personal health besides the traditional periodic visits to the doctor for scheduled checkups or upon sickness. This is an important application area for multimodal data integration and abstraction of sensor data, and for diagnosis and remedial action [Henson et al., 2011]. Figure 9.2 depicts background knowledge encoded as bipartite graph capturing manifestations (symptoms) associated with two common disorders (diseases) - flu and cold [Henson et al., 2012a]. Measurements from a thermometer can be abstracted to determine fever while other symptoms can be obtained by interviewing or examining the patient. In general, if the observed symptoms are insufficient for actionable diagnosis, it is necessary to infer promising hypotheses, and make necessary additional observations, in order to decide on a remedial course of action.

Figure 9.3 illustrates how perception cycles can be used to narrow down the five possible explanations (that is, panic disorder, hypoglycemia, hyperthyroidism, heart attack, and septic shock) of the two observed symptoms (that is, abnormal heart rate and clammy skin), by systematically

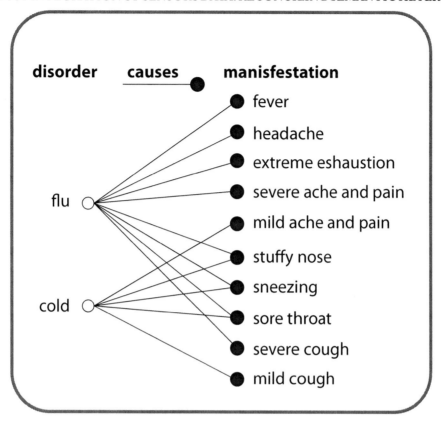

Figure 9.2: Medical background knowledge in the form of bipartite graph relating disorders and their manifestations [Henson et al., 2012a] (copyright © IEEE, with permission).

seeking additional symptoms (through appropriate questioning in this case), to obtain the diagnosis, and eventually, prescription medications and alerts.

Semantic Web technologies can be harnessed to build systems that can assimilate and interpret sensor data. To achieve this, we can semantically annotate the raw sensor data using RDF, employing named relationships from the Semantic Sensor Network (SSN) ontology [Compton et al., 2012]. SSN ontology enables representation and sharing of descriptions of sensor devices, systems, processes, and observations on the Web. These semantically annotated sensor observation data can be translated into abstractions using perception cycle captured through IntellegO [Henson et al., 2011, 2012a]. IntellegO, an ontology of perception, is a formal model that encompasses both machine perception and human perception. It formalizes (i) background knowledge in the form of bipartite graph involving *entities* and *qualities*, and (ii) *perception cycle* to *explain* a set of qualities in terms of a set of entities, and to seek additional *discriminating* qualities that can assist in minimizing explanation.

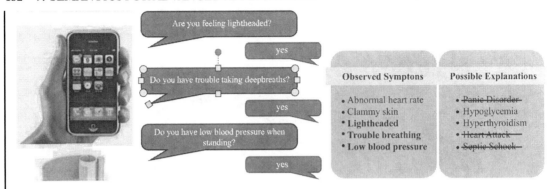

Figure 9.3: Perception cycle to seek additional symptoms in order to determine the diagnosis [Henson et al., 2012a] (copyright © IEEE, with permission).

To go from small-scale prototype to a full-scale deployment in the health care domain requires overcoming several practical challenges including:

1. *Expressive semantic representation*: The faithful representation of concepts and their relationships reflecting contextual constraints is complex and difficult to codify.

2. *Data quality*: The validation of sensor observations is necessary to ensure high-quality data. In the presence of uncertainty, it is necessary to reflect it in the diagnosis, to gauge its fidelity.

3. *Comprehensibility*: The determination and easy-to-grasp summarization of patient's health condition, and synthesis of informative alerts for further action to patient and clinician, is non-trivial.

The dramatic advances and adoption of sensor technologies to monitor us and our environment, to promote health and well-being, has led to increasing embedding of sensors within mobile devices or providing bio-metric sensors access to mobile devices through either physical attachments or wireless communication protocols, such as Bluetooth. Their wide spread uptake in practice requires development of efficient algorithms for semantics-based machine perception in resource-constrained devices (among other things). Henson et al. [2012b] demonstrate a simple, effective, and scalable approach. In particular, the work presents three contributions: (1) a simple declarative specification (in OWL) of two inference tasks useful for machine perception, explanation, and discrimination; (2) efficient algorithms for these inference tasks, using bit vector operations; and (3) lifting and lowering mappings to enable the translation of knowledge between semantic representations and the bit vector representations. The bit vector encodings and algorithms yield *significant* and *necessary* computational enhancements—including asymptotic order of magnitude improvement, with running times reduced from several minutes to milliseconds, and problem size increased from 10's to 1,000's. The approach has been prototyped and evaluated on a mobile device, with promising applications of contemporary relevance (e.g., healthcare/cardiology).

9.2   SPATIO-TEMPORAL SLICING AND THEMATIC FILTERING: ACHIEVING SCALABILITY

The emergence of microblogging platforms, such as Twitter, FriendFeed, and Jaiku, has revolutionized how unfiltered, real-time information is disseminated and consumed by citizens. Perhaps, the most interesting phenomenon about such data is that they act as a lens into the social perception of an event in any region, at any point in time. Citizen observations about the same event relayed from the same or different location offer multiple, complementary viewpoints or storylines about an event. Furthermore, these viewpoints evolve over time, and influence regional neighborhoods. Consequently, in addition to what is being said about an event (theme), where (spatial) and when (temporal) it is said, are critical and integral components to the meaningful analysis of such data. Citizen sensor observations are inherently multidimensional in nature and taking these dimensions into account, while processing, aggregating, connecting, and visualizing data will provide useful organization and consumption principles.

In order to profit from the glut of real-time machine and citizen sensor data, it is necessary to analyze and abstract data for the information seekers and decision makers in a form that is both intelligible and timely. To improve computational efficiency, it is necessary to glean uniformity and parallelism in both computations and data, and employ cloud computing infrastructure for data analytics. To improve quality of abstraction, it is necessary to glean semantically and contextually relevant information and present it in a form that is suitable for decision makers. Spatio-temporal information available as a part of metadata associated with sensor data can be exploited to partition the data into independent slices amenable to parallel/distributed processing.

For a detailed example, consider the Twitris application [Nagarajan et al., 2009b] that (i) extracts social signals for understanding connections between people, places, and events, (ii) uses spatio-temporal-thematic metadata extracted from the tweets to summarize the semantic content and sentiments [Chen et al., 2012], (iii) creates a mashup for visualizing the spatio-temporal-thematic (STT) aspects, and (iv) provides a foundation for exploring other news and multimedia information sources. Twitris starts with a static set of tweets about an event, partitions it into subsets based on spatio-temporal information associated with the tweets and the nature of the event, and processes each *spatio-temporal slice* (STS) similarly. For example, tweets can be partitioned into STSs based on two tunable parameters - the spatial parameter δs and the temporal parameter δt, arrived at to capture coherence and appropriate level of granularity for analysis. δs can be defined to cover a spatial region such as a country, a state, and a city, and δt can be defined to cover time intervals such as hours, days, and weeks. For the Haiti earthquake, one might look at country-level activity on a daily basis, and for presidential election, one might look at state-level activity on a weekly basis. Event descriptors, which summarize a spatio-temporal slice of tweets, are in the form of statistically significant N-grams that have been extracted from the tweets. This is computationally very demanding and its sequential implementation is the bottleneck to its scalability. Furthermore, while a corpus of tweets can go a long way in determining event descriptors, the variability and creativity of expression makes the statistics solely drawn from a corpus of tweets inadequate to yield quality event descriptors. In order to significantly improve Twitris' scalability and quality for providing social perception, it is necessary to perform more fine-grained, real-time analysis of tweets, and employ better data-intensive, contemporary language models to mirror the inherently dynamic and informal nature of tweet text. To improve computational/syntactic scalability, cloud computing infrastructures have been employed, and to improve its quality/semantic scalability, principled approaches to characterizing significant event descriptors and domain semantics to obtain an appropriate language model have been explored. In all these, there are obvious sources of parallelism—structural homogeneity in data and locality in computation. STT analysis of different events is independent. N-grams extraction, their thematic scoring, and the selection of event descriptors for different STSs, are all independent and inherently parallelizable. Within each STS, N-grams extraction and portions of computation for thematic scoring are embarrassingly parallel. In contrast, the spatio-temporal discounting of the thematic score of an N-gram requires interaction among neighboring STSs for aggregation and filtering of information to modulate its score. Fortunately, even these operations exhibit bounded locality. For concreteness, in the jargon of *map-reduce paradigm*, local computations can be encapsulated to yield *mappers*, global aggregation computations can be encapsulated to yield *reducers*, and local aggregation computations (such as selecting top-k values) can be encapsulated to yield *combiners* [Yahoo, 2012]. Furthermore, these computations can be weaved together into a complete workflow.

In the context of making sensor data easy to query from a user's perspective, semantically rich LOD and domain models can be exploited. Recall that the Linked Data consists of interlinked public datasets encoded in RDF that spans diverse areas such as life sciences, astronomy, sensors, geography, and entertainment. While accessing sensor data, users would like to formulate queries in terms of concepts that are natural to them, and expect results, in a timely manner, that are concise and easy to comprehend. For instance, in the context of weather domain, this translates to being able to use geographical names in the query and being able to obtain real-time reports on the weather situation in qualitative terms (using weather features) such as cloudy, clear, or ice storm, rather than in numerical terms (using weather phenomena values) such as temperature, precipitation, or wind speed values. This requires conversion of geographical names into location attributes such as latitude, longitude, and elevation, to determine the nearest weather station, and abstracting weather phenomenon values to weather feature values as defined by NOAA. *In essence, there is need for syntactic scalability to enable real-time analysis of large datasets, and for semantic scalability to enable end-user digest the data, to base decisions* [Henson et al., 2011, Sheth et al., 2008b]. In fact, another burgeoning area of research is the development of hybrid cloud mobile applications that use cloud infrastructure as the backend for computations and mobile devices as the front-end for sensing and display, with domain-specific languages used to deal with heterogeneity at the two ends [Ranabahu et al., 2010, 2011b].

In summary, as additional sensor datasets and ontologies come online, harnessing it using mobile devices in innovative ways will require exploitation of syntactic and semantic scalability through the application of spatio-temporal-thematic semantics.

9.3   DYNAMIC MODEL CREATION AND UPDATE: CONTINUOUS SEMANTICS

Typically, domain experts build ontologies by formalizing domain concepts and relationships, and populating ontologies using facts from the corpus of background knowledge. Ontologies are applied to extract semantic metadata or to semantically annotate data in a new corpora, or to reason with them. This approach works well for slowly evolving knowledge, where the primary purpose is to obtain broad community-wide commitment to shared world view and vocabulary. Unfortunately, this approach has its limitations when processing dynamic domains involved in social, mobile, and sensor webs, where normalization for real-time machine-processing is an important concern. Specifically, social/citizen sensor data are spontaneous, rapidly changing, and potentially diverse in content and opinions. Thus, a domain model that does not significantly lag behind the actual events, which are the subject matter of the sensed data, is crucial for accurate classification and content assimilation. We prefer the term 'domain model' to 'ontology' in this context because the latter has connotation of being rigorous and human-mediated while our focus is on agility and automation even if approximate.

Continuous semantics refers to the idea of building domain models by pruning community-created background knowledge iteratively in response to newly acquired focus from the data stream. Continuous semantics aims to make domain models responsive to changes by respecting and automatically harnessing available community-based consensus. Ultimately, this should enable more meaningful filtering and annotation of real-time data streams. For example, in the context of natural disaster related Twitter data stream, the discussion focus can shift frequently as the event unfolds, from initial response, to rescue to recovery to rehabilitation; their comprehension requires concomitant change to the background domain model.

In practice, continuous semantics can be realized using sensor data stream such as tweets from Twitter and community-created knowledge such as Wikipedia [Sheth et al., 2010]. Wikipedia, barring its news component, is an up-to-date collection of encyclopedic knowledge. When a page is updated in response to new information, it is well-integrated with existing content. The way Wikipedia gracefully assimilates the coverage of new events makes it a good candidate source for knowledge from which to create domain models. Its category structure crudely resembles a formal ontology's class hierarchy, even though many subcategory relationships in Wikipedia are associative rather than strict subclass or type relationships.

The Doozer project developed a probabilistic approach to iteratively "expand and reduce" the knowledge space from user-supplied seed key phrases, to create focused domain models of evolving and changing domains [Thomas et al., 2008]. Figure 9.4 from Sheth et al. [2010] illustrates the four steps required to realize and utilize continuous semantics: (a) real-time data are queried and filtered to find event-specific content; (b) the data are abstracted and analyzed to extract notable entities and social signals; (c) domain models and background knowledge are dynamically and contextually created to allow additional semantic analysis for identifying meaningful concepts and their relationships; and (d) the new concepts are then used to continue processing of real-time content using enriched background knowledge for further querying and filtering.

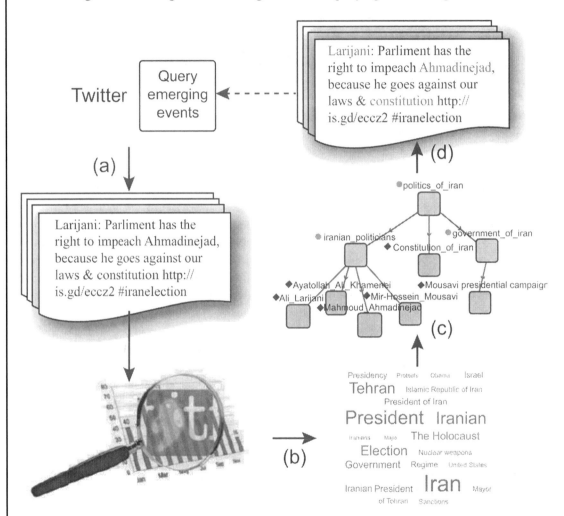

Figure 9.4: A pipeline for real-time data analysis using continuous semantics [Sheth et al., 2010] (Copyright © IEEE, with permission).

To illustrate the feasibility of the above approach, the entire pipeline has been implemented using Twitter and Twitris [Nagarajan et al., 2009b] (which extracts social signals from tweets related to events and emergent situations), Twarql [Mendes et al., 2010] (which can query annotated tweets stream), and Doozer (which creates dynamic domain models). Tweets related to a specific event—in this case, the Iranian election (see Figure 9.4a)—is automatically identified using hash tags and keywords associated with that event using the Twitter API. Thematic analysis by Twitris gives a set of N-grams or key phrases exemplified by the tag cloud in Figure 9.4b. Doozer uses key phrases to automatically and dynamically create a model from Wikipedia and other qualified sources such as Freebase (see Figure 9.4c). Twitris uses the domain model to semantically annotate and support semantic analysis of the original tweets (as in Figure 9.4a) and subsequent tweets (see Figure 9.4d). It does this by restricting Twarql annotations of streaming data to the domain spanned by the model. Twitris can then identify new keywords and hash tags to expand or can modify semantic processing as the event evolves. This in turn leads to new key phrases for dynamic model extraction and updating. However, by this time the underlying Wikipedia pages or other qualified social-knowledge sources might have been updated. This updating will yield new concepts in an evolved domain model that reflects the real-world changes being analyzed. Also, Twitris's thematic-analysis component can consider as new input the entities that are annotated using the Doozer output hierarchy. This creates a feedback loop between content analysis and model evolution. Figure 9.5 (taken from Sheth et al. [2010]) shows a part of Doozer-created domain model representing Iranian politics, and the mapping of entities to words and phrases in tweets (that is, semantic annotation of tweets).

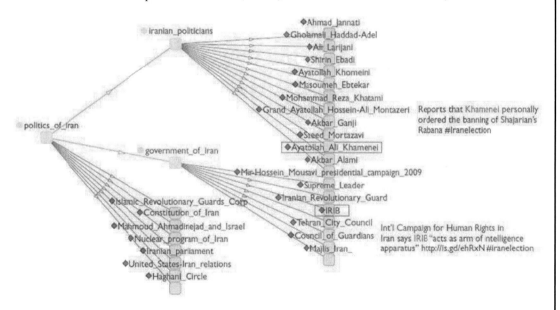

Figure 9.5: An excerpt of the model focusing on the Iranian government and politicians. [Sheth et al., 2010] (Copyright © IEEE, with permission).

Such semantic processing of real-time (textual) data shares the technological underpinnings of the SSW [Mendes et al., 2010, Sheth et al., 2008b]. Combining the two can lead to integrated semantic analysis of multimodal data streams. On-demand creation of semantic models from social-knowledge sources such as Wikipedia offers exciting new opportunities for making real-time social and sensor data more meaningful and useful for advanced situational-awareness and situational-analysis applications.

9.4   ROLE OF SEMANTICS IN WEB OF THINGS (CYBER-PHYSICAL SYSTEMS)

The agenda of the Web of Things (WoT) or Internet of Things (IoT) is to connect ordinary objects (with embedded sensors and actuators, communication and networking capabilities) to the Web for remote access, monitoring, and control. Realization of WoT requires convergence of scalable technologies for economical device miniaturization and integration, wireless networking, and robust intelligent system which can be founded on Semantic Web.

Consider a sampling of applications for WoT of varying degrees of criticality and complexity [Fortuna and Grobelnik, 2011].

1. Obtaining map of radiation levels in a nuclear disaster area, or map of water logging as a result of floods.

2. Developing objects that communicate their status periodically, or driven by specific events or needs. For example, utility meters can send out monthly readings, "exotic" houseplants can demand water, and online laundry service can minimize wait times.

3. Monitoring and controlling components of public utility systems (such as power grid, transportation, and water distribution), roads and bridges, smart homes, environment and personal healthcare for various reasons including energy efficiency, load distribution, logistics, maintenance, traceability, problem diagnosis, and improving quality of life.

4. Smart LED-equipped wine rack can provide owner the inventory, or assist in wine selection by lighting up LED for queried bottles.[1] This can be generalized to inventory control in a warehouse, or shopping assistant in a super market or a department store.

Semantics is needed to provide proper context and interpretation of the sensed data. For specificity and for illustration purposes, consider the semantic streams framework for transforming raw sensor data into real-world objects and events, by utilizing background knowledge [Whitehouse et al., 2006]. Four break beam sensors in a parking garage can be used to determine if a parking spot is free or occupied. Quoting Whitehouse et al. [2006]: "Break beam sensors, motion sensors and magnetometers can be configured to infer the presence of humans, motorcycles and cars as well as their speeds, directions, sizes, metallic payloads and, in combination with data from neighboring locations, even their paths through the parking garage." This information can be used (i) for real-time analysis such as to determine and take pictures of vehicles moving faster than the

---

[1]http://www.bbc.co.uk/news/business-13632206

speed limit, or to detect suspicious activity, and (ii) for offline analysis to understand the nature and variation of parking garage traffic and occupancy over the entire day or week.

In order to realize WoT, we need a mechanism to directly or indirectly Web-enable objects ("things") and then process the sensed heterogeneous data for status monitoring or decision making as sanctioned by their semantics and context. SemSOS [Henson et al., 2009] enriches the SOS by leveraging semantic technologies (such as URL, HTTP, RDF, REST) in order to provide and apply more meaningful representation of sensor data. More specifically, it enables modeling the domain of sensors and sensor observations in a suite of ontologies [Sheth, 2010], adding semantic annotations to the sensor data, using the ontology models to abstract and reason over sensor observations. In the end, SemSOS provides the ability to query high-level knowledge about the objects and the events as well as low-level raw sensor data.

9.4.1   SEMANTICS EMPOWERED PHYSICAL-CYBER-SOCIAL SYSTEMS

The role of semantics for interoperability, integration, and improved querying has been investigated for a few decades. Semantic systems built using informal and implicit forms of semantics are more commonplace than those using formal Semantic Web languages and mainstream Semantic Web technologies. This is because the Web is increasingly becoming diffused and incidental (e.g., more people access content through applications compared to the Web browsers), and lighter-weight approaches have led to better developer and user engagements, and scalable applications. Apple Siri, IBM Watson, and Google Knowledge Graph are representative of the current trend that also excel at using light-weight (that is, focused on using vocabularies and relationships but not formal languages like OWL) semantics at scale. Simultaneously, Web is increasingly merging with other powerful technologies that support semantics, including machine learning, NLP, and knowledge-based systems where background knowledge is applied.

Computing for Human Experience vision is about employing a suite of technologies to nondestructively and unobtrusively complement and enrich normal human activities, with minimal explicit concern or effort on the humans' part [Sheth]. It has a long lineage, starting in part with Vannevar Bush's Memex [Bush, 1945] through Mark Weiser's "Computing in the 21st Century" [Weiser, 1991] and others. The coming decade will see unique opportunities with the evolution of physical-cyber-social systems that will involve the following (among several other) areas of significant progress:

- Making human interaction with technology very natural (e.g., gesture computing); blur the differences between human's physical, cyber, and social presence by bridging the physical and digital divide.

- Incorporating powerful ways the human brain works into the fabric of computing and communication (significant progress from neuroscience to cognitive science, and the resulting ability to model and mimic the human brain or thinking processes).

- Bringing the physical world, cyberspace, and human closer with the help of devices around, on, and inside the human body.

- Continuously and dynamically create collective intelligence and background knowledge, combine that with historical and common sense knowledge, and contextually apply relevant knowledge and experiences to enhance technological support at all levels of physical-cyber-social systems (i.e., continuous semantics [Sheth et al., 2010]).

In a nutshell, we expect semantics to be a key enabler of Computing for Human Experience [Sheth, 2010].

Bibliography

R. Agrawal and R. Srikant. Fast algorithms for mining association rules. In *Proc. 20th Int. Conf. on Very Large Data Bases*, pages 487–499, 1994. DOI: 10.1109/CCECE.2002.1013116 Cited on page(s) 18

R. Agrawal, T. Imieliński, and A. Swami. Mining association rules between sets of items in large databases. In *Proc. ACM SIGMOD Int. Conf. on Management of Data*, pages 207–216, 1993. DOI: 10.1145/170036.170072 Cited on page(s) 18

R. Akkiraju, J. Farrell, J. Miller, M. Nagarajan, M. Schmidt, A. Sheth, and K. Verma. Web service semantics-WSDL-S. W3C Member Submission, 2005. URL http://www.w3.org/Submission/WSDL-S/. Cited on page(s) 70, 72

A. Alba, V. Bhagwan, J. Grace, D. Gruhl, K. Haas, M. Nagarajan, J. Pieper, C. Robson, and N. Sahoo. Applications of voting theory to information mashups. In *Proc. 2nd IEEE Int. Conf. on Semantic Computing*, pages 10–17, 2008. DOI: 10.1109/ICSC.2008.78 Cited on page(s) 106

B. Aleman-meza, A. Sheth, M. Eavenson, and I. B. Arpinar. Semantic analytics in intelligence: Applying semantic association discovery to determine relevance of heterogeneous documents. In Keng Siau, editor, *Advanced Topics in Database Research*, volume 5, pages 401–419. Idea Publishers, 2006. DOI: 10.4018/978-1-59140-935-9 Cited on page(s) 51

D. Allemang. Semantic web and the linked data enterprise linking enterprise data. In *Linking Enterprise Data*, chapter 1, pages 3–23. Springer, 2010. DOI: 10.1007/978-1-4419-7665-9_1 Cited on page(s) 50

G. Antoniou and F. van Harmelen. *A Semantic Web Primer*. MIT Press, 2004. Cited on page(s) 6

K Anyanwu and A. P. Sheth. The ρ operator: Discovering and ranking associations on the semantic web. *ACM SIGMOD Rec.*, 31(4):42–47, 2002. DOI: 10.1145/637411.637418 Cited on page(s) 18, 38

Apache. Apache uima, 2012. URL http://uima.apache.org. Cited on page(s) 36

M. Arenas, A. Bertails, E. Prud'hommeaux, and J. Sequeda. A direct mapping of relational data to RDF. W3C Recommendation, 2012. URL http://www.w3.org/TR/2012/NOTE-microdata-rdf-20121009/. Cited on page(s) 48

D. Atkins. Revolutionizing science and engineering through cyberinfrastructure. Report of the National Science Foundation Blue-ribbon Advisory Panel on Cyberinfrastructure, 2003. Cited on page(s) 50

D. Avant, M. Baum, C. Bertram, M. Fisher, A. Sheth, and Y. Warke. Semantic technology applications for homeland security. In *Proc. 11th Int. Conf. on Information and Knowledge Management*, pages 611–613, 2002. DOI: 10.1145/584792.584893 Cited on page(s) 62

F. Baader. *The Description Logic Handbook: Theory, Implementation, and Applications.* Cambridge University Press, 2003. Cited on page(s) 11, 18

C. Baker and K. Cheung. *Semantic Web: Revolutionizing Knowledge Discovery in the Life Sciences.* Springer, 2007. Cited on page(s) 62

T. Berners Lee. Linked data, 2006. URL http://www.w3.org/DesignIssues/LinkedData. html. Cited on page(s) 26

T. Berners-Lee and M. Fischetti. *Weaving the Web: The Original Design and Ultimate Destiny of the World Wide Web by its Inventor.* DIANE Publishing Company, 2001. Cited on page(s) 6

H Blair and V. Subrahmanian. Paraconsistent logic programming. *Theor. Comp. Sci.*, 68(2):135–154, 1989. DOI: 10.1016/0304-3975(89)90126-6 Cited on page(s) 15

O. Bodenreider. The unified medical language system : What is it and how to use it? 2007. URL http://www.slideshare.net/roger961/the-unified-medical-language-system-what-is-it-and-how-to-use-it. Cited on page(s) 25

M. Botts, G. Percivall, C. Reed, and J. Davidson. Ogc® sensor web enablement: Overview and high level architecture. In *Proc. 2nd Int. Conf. GeoSensor Networks*, pages 175–190, 2008. Cited on page(s) 87

S. Brin and L. Page. The anatomy of a large-scale hypertextual web search engine. In *Proc. 7th Int. World Wide Web Conf.*, pages 107–117, 1998. DOI: 10.1016/S0169-7552(98)00110-X Cited on page(s) 17

V. Bush. As we may think. *The Atlantic*, July 1945. URL http://www.theatlantic.com/magazine/archive/1945/07/as-we-may-think/3881/. Cited on page(s) 139

T. Cao. Annotated fuzzy logic programs. *Fuzzy Sets and Systems*, 113(2):277–298, 2000. DOI: 10.1016/S0165-0114(98)00083-9 Cited on page(s) 15

J. Cardoso, A. Sheth, J. Miller, J. Arnold, and K. Kochut. Quality of service for workflows and web service processes. *J. Web Semantics*, 1(3):281–308, 2004. DOI: 10.1016/j.websem.2004.03.001 Cited on page(s) 68

J. Cardoso, M. Hepp, and M. D. Lytras. *The Semantic Web: Real-World Applications from Industry*, volume 6 of *Semantic Web And Beyond Computing for Human Experience*. Springer, 2007. Cited on page(s) 62

M. Carrara and N. Guarino. Formal ontology and conceptual analysis: a structured bibliography. 1999. URL http://www.pms.informatik.unimuenchen.de/mitarbeiter/ohlbach/Ontology/Ontobiblio.doc. Cited on page(s) 50

B. Chandrasekaran, J. Josephson, and V. Benjamins. What are ontologies, and why do we need them? *IEEE Internet Comput.*, 14(1):20–26, 1999. DOI: 10.1109/5254.747902 Cited on page(s) 28

F. Chang, J. Dean, S. Ghemawat, W.C. Hsieh, D.A. Wallach, M. Burrows, T. Chandra, A. Fikes, and R.E. Gruber. BigTable: A distributed storage system for structured data. *ACM Trans. Comp. Syst.*, 26(2):4:1–4:26, 2008. Cited on page(s) 119

S. Charlton. Elastra, oopsla workshop "designing for the cloud", 2009. URL http://www.slideshare.net/StuC/oopsla-cloud-workshop-designing-for-the-cloud-elastra. Cited on page(s) 118

L. Chen, W. Wang, M. Nagarajan, S. Wang, and A.P. Sheth. Extracting diverse sentiment expressions with target-dependent polarity from twitter. In *Proc. 6th Int. AAAI Conf. on Weblogs and Social Media*, pages 50–57, 2012. Cited on page(s) 133

T. Chklovski and P. Pantel. VerbOcean: Mining the web for fine-grained semantic verb relations. In *Proc. Conf. on Empirical Methods in Natural Language Processing*, pages 33–40, 2004. Cited on page(s) 26

E.F. Codd. A relational model of data for large shared data banks. *Commun. ACM*, 13(6):377–387, 1970. DOI: 10.1145/362384.362685 Cited on page(s) 19

M. Compton, P. Barnaghi, L. Bermudez, R. Garcia-Castro, O. Corcho, S. Cox, J. Graybeal, M. Hauswirth, C. Henson, and A. Herzog. The SSN ontology of the W3C semantic sensor network incubator group. *J. Web Semantics*, 2012. DOI: 10.1016/j.websem.2012.05.003 Cited on page(s) 91, 131

D. Connoly. Gleaning resource descriptions from dialects of languages (GRDDL). W3C Recommendation, 2007. URL http://www.w3.org/TR/grddl/. Cited on page(s) 12, 48

R. L. Costello and T. D. Kehoe. Rest, 2005. URL http://www.slideshare.net/gfarid/rest-full-11933692. Cited on page(s) 64

N. Dalvi, R. Kumar, B. Pang, R. Ramakrishnan, A. Tomkins, P. Bohannon, S. Keerthi, and S. Merugu. A web of concepts. In *Proc. 28th ACM SIGACT-SIGMOD-SIGART Symp. on Principles of Database Systems*, pages 1–12, 2009. DOI: 10.1145/1559795.1559797 Cited on page(s) 51

S. Das, S. Sundara, and R. Cyganiak. R2RML: RDB to RDF mapping language. W3C Recommendation, 2012. URL http://www.w3.org/TR/r2rml/. Cited on page(s) 48

S. Dill, N. Eiron, D. G. Daniel Gruhl, R. V. Guha, A. Jhingran, T. Kanungo, S. Rajagopalan, and A. Tomkins. SemTag and Seeker: Bootstrapping the semantic web via automated semantic annotation. In *Proc. 12th Int. World Wide Web Conf.*, pages 178–186, 2003. DOI: 10.1145/775152.775178 Cited on page(s) 13, 58

J. Domingue, D. Fensel, and J. Hendler. *Handbook of Semantic Web Technologies*. Springer, 2011. DOI: 10.1007/978-3-540-92913-0 Cited on page(s) 6

D. M. Dubois, G. Resconi, and A. Raymondi. TurboBrain: A neural network with direct learning based on linear or non-linear threshold logics. In *Proc. 4th Int. Workshop Computer Aided Systems Theory*, pages 278–294, 1994. DOI: 10.1007/3-540-61478-8_83 Cited on page(s) 14

D Evans. The internet of things – how the next evolution of the internet is changing everything. CISCO White Paper, 2011. Available at http://www.cisco.com/web/about/ac79/docs/innov/IoT_IBSG_0411FINAL.pdf. Cited on page(s) 83

Facebook. The open graph, 2011. URL http://developers.facebook.com/docs/opengraph/. Cited on page(s) 43

C. Fellbaum. *WordNet: An Electronic Lexical Database*. The MIT Press, 1998. Cited on page(s) 23

D. Fensel. *Ontologies: A Silver Bullet for Knowledge Management and Electronic-Commerce*. Spring-Verlag, 2000. DOI: 10.1145/637411.637425 Cited on page(s) 16

D. Ferrucci, E. Brown, J. Chu-Carroll, J. Fan, D. Gondek, A. Kalyanpur, A. Lally, J. Murdock, E. Nyberg, and et al. J. Prager. Building Watson: An overview of the DeepQA project. *AI Magazine*, 31(3):59–79, 2010. Cited on page(s) 17

R. Fielding. *Architectural Styles and the Design of Network-based Software Architectures*. PhD thesis, University of California, 2000. Cited on page(s) 45, 64

C. Fortuna and M. Grobelnik. The web of things tutorial. In *8th Extended Semantic Web Conference*, 2011. DOI: 10.1145/1963192.1963320 Cited on page(s) 138

F. Giunchiglia and I. Zaihrayeu. Lightweight ontologies. Technical Report DIT-07-071, University of Trento, 2007. URL http://eprints.biblio.unitn.it/1289/1/071.pdf. Cited on page(s) 33

C. Goble. Position statement: Musings on provenance, workflow and (semantic web) annotations for bioinformatics. In *Proc. Workshop on Data Derivation and Provenance*, 2002. Cited on page(s) 57

C. Goble, R. Stevens, and S. Bechhofer. The semantic web and knowledge grids. *Drug Discovery Today: Technologies*, 2(3):225–233, 2005. DOI: 10.1016/j.ddtec.2005.08.005 Cited on page(s) 62

J. Golbeck, A. Mannes, and J. Hendler. Semantic web technologies for terrorist network analysis. In Robert L. Popp and John Yen, editors, *Emergent Information Technologies and Enabling Policies for Counter-Terrorism*, chapter 6, pages 125–137. Wiley, 2006. DOI: 10.1002/047178656X Cited on page(s) 62

J. Grace, D. Gruhl, K. Haas, M. Nagarajan, C. Robson, and N. Sahoo. Artist ranking through analysis of on-line community comments. Unpublished manuscript, 2007. URL http://knoesis.wright.edu/library/resource.php?id=00176. Cited on page(s) 103

N. Gross. The earth will don an electronic skin. *Business Week*, 1999. URL http://www.businessweek.com/1999/99_35/b3644024.htm. Cited on page(s) 97

T. Gruber. It is what it does: The pragmatics of ontology. Invited presentation to the meeting of the CIDOC Conceptual Reference Model Committee, Smithsonian Museum. Available at http://cidoc.ics.forth.gr/docs/symposium_presentations/gruber_cidoc-ontology-2003.pdf, 2003. Cited on page(s) 12, 28, 60

T. Gruber. Ontology of folksonomy: A mash-up of apples and oranges. *J. Semantic Web and Information Systems*, 3(1):1–11, 2007. DOI: 10.4018/jswis.2007010101 Cited on page(s) 24

T. Gruber. What is an ontology. In L. Liu and M. T. Özsu, editors, *Encyclopedia of Database Systems*. Springer, 2008. Cited on page(s) 27, 29

T.R. Gruber. Toward principles for the design of ontologies used for knowledge sharing. *Int. J. of Human Computer Studies*, 43(5):907–928, 1995. DOI: 10.1006/ijhc.1995.1081 Cited on page(s) 5, 27

D. Gruhl, M. Nagarajan, J. Pieper, C. Robson, and A. Sheth. Multimodal social intelligence in a real-time dashboard system. *VLDB J.*, 19(6):825–848, 2010. DOI: 10.1007/s00778-010-0207-5 Cited on page(s) 106, 108

M. Gruninger and M.S. Fox. Methodology for the design and evaluation of ontologies. In *Proc. Workshop on Basic Ontological Issues in Knowledge Sharing*, 1995. Cited on page(s) 29

P. Gu. Causal knowledge modeling for traditional chinese medicine using OWL 2. In *Proc. 9th Int. Semantic Web Conf.*, 2010. Cited on page(s) 27

N. Guarino. Formal ontology in information systems. In *Proc. 1st Int. Conf. on Formal Ontology in Information Systems*, pages 6–8, 1998. Cited on page(s) 28

N. Guarino, M. Carrara, and P. Giaretta. An ontology of meta-level categories. In *Proc. 4th Int. Conf. Principles of Knowledge Representation and Reasoning*, pages 270–280, 1994. Cited on page(s) 31

A. Gugliotta, J. Domingue, L. Cabral, V. Tanasescu, S. Galizia, R. Davies, L. Villarias, M. Rowlatt, M. Richardson, and S. Stincic. Deploying semantic web services-based applications in the e-government domain. *J. Data Semantics*, 10:96–132, 2008. DOI: 10.1007/978-3-540-77688-8_4 Cited on page(s) 82

R. Guha, R. McCool, and E. Miller. Semantic search. In *Proc. 12th Int. World Wide Web Conf.*, pages 700–709, 2003. DOI: 10.1145/775152.775250 Cited on page(s) 17

B. Gustavsson. On the semantic web language. Technical Report 01065, Växjö University, 2001. URL http://home.swipnet.se/semanticweb/thesis/index.html. Cited on page(s) 28

J. Guttag, J. Horning, W. Garl, K. Jones, A. Modet, and J. Wing. Larch: Languages and tools for formal specification. *Texts and Monographs in Computer Science*, 1993. Cited on page(s) 19

A. Halevy. Why your data won't mix. *ACM Queue*, 3(8):51–58, 2005. DOI: 10.1145/1103822.1103836 Cited on page(s) 130

H. Halpin and I. Davis. GRDDL primer. W3C Working Group Note, 2007. URL http://www.w3.org/TR/grddl-primer/. Cited on page(s) 12, 48

B. Hammond, A. Sheth, and K. Kochut. Semantic enhancement engine: A modular document enhancement platform for semantic applications over heterogeneous content. In V. Kashyap and L. Shklar, editors, *Real World Semantic Web Applications*, pages 29–49. IOS Press, 2002. Cited on page(s) 52, 58

M. Hausenblas, I. Herman, and B. Adida. RDFa-bridging the web of documents and the web of data. In *Tutorial at 7th Int. Semantic Web Conf.*, 2008. URL http://www.w3.org/2008/Talks/1026-ISCW-RDFa/RDFa-ISWC08.html. Cited on page(s) 12, 42

J. Heinsohn. Probabilistic description logics. In *Proc. 10th Int. Conf. on Uncertainty in Artificial Intelligence*, pages 311–318, 1994. Cited on page(s) 15

C. Henson, A. Sheth, P. Jain, J. Pschorr, and T. Rapoch. Video on the semantic sensor web. In *Proc. W3C Video on the Web Workshop*, 2007. URL http://www.w3.org/2007/08/video/positions/Wright.pdf. DOI: 10.1007/978-3-642-02121-3_3 Cited on page(s) 92

C. Henson, J. Pschorr, A. Sheth, and K. Thirunarayan. SemSOS: Semantic sensor observation service. In *Proc. Int. Symp. on Collaborative Technologies and Systems*, pages 18–22, 2009. DOI: 10.1109/CTS.2009.5067461 Cited on page(s) 92, 94, 139

C. Henson, K. Thirunarayan, and A. Sheth. An ontological approach to focusing attention and enhancing machine perception on the web. *Applied Ontology*, 6(4):345–376, 2011. DOI: 10.3233/AO-2011-0100 Cited on page(s) 15, 130, 131, 134

C. Henson, A. Sheth, and K. Thirunarayan. Semantic perception: Converting sensory observations to abstractions. *IEEE Internet Comput.*, 16(2):26–34, 2012a. DOI: 10.1109/MIC.2012.20 Cited on page(s) 130, 131, 132

C. Henson, K. Thirunarayan, and A. Sheth. An efficient bit vector approach to semantics-based machine perception in resource-constrained devices. In *Proc. 11th Int. Semantic Web Conf.*, pages 149–164, 2012b. DOI: 10.1007/978-3-642-35176-1_10 Cited on page(s) 132

T. Hey and A. Trefethen. Cyberinfrastructure for e-science. *Science*, 308:817–821, 2005. DOI: 10.1126/science.1110410 Cited on page(s) 50

I. Hickson. Html microdata. Technical Report WD-microdata-20110525, World Wide Web Consortium, Working Draft, 2011. URL http://www.w3.org/TR/2011/WD-microdata-20110405/. Cited on page(s) 42, 44

I. Hickson, G. Kellogg, J. Tennison, and I. Herman. Microdata to RDF : Transformation from HTML+Microdata to RDF. W3C Recommendation, 2012. URL http://www.w3.org/TR/2012/NOTE-microdata-rdf-20121009/. Cited on page(s) 45

P. Hitzler, M. Krötzsch, B. Parsia, P.F. Patel-Schneider, and S. Rudolph. OWL 2 web ontology language primer. W3C recommendation, 2009a. URL http://www.w3.org/TR/owl2-primer/. Cited on page(s) 11

P. Hitzler, M. Krötzsch, and S. Rudolph. *Foundations of Semantic Web Technologies*. Chapman & Hall/CRC, 2009b. Cited on page(s) 11, 18

J. R. Hobbs and F. Pan. An ontology of time for the semantic web. *ACM Trans. Asian Lang. Information Proc.*, 3:66–85, 2004. DOI: 10.1145/1017068.1017073 Cited on page(s) 89

D. Huynh and S. Mazzocchi. Google refine, 2011. Available at:http://en.wikipedia.org/wiki/Google_Refine. Cited on page(s) 59, 70

IBM. Bringing big data to the enterprise, 2012. URL http://www-01.ibm.com/software/data/bigdata/. Cited on page(s) 83

K. Idehen. Kingsley idehen's blog data space, 2012. http://www.openlinksw.com/dataspace/kidehen@openlinksw.com/weblog/kidehen@openlinksw.com%27s%20BLOG%20%5B127%5D/1531. Cited on page(s) 5

M. Jaeger. Probabilistic reasoning in terminological logics. In *Proc. 4th Int. Conf. Principles of Knowledge Representation and Reasoning*, pages 305–316, 1994. Cited on page(s) 15

P. Jain, P. Yeh, K. Verma, C. Henson, and A. Sheth. SPARQL query re-writing using partonomy based transformation rules. In *Proc. 3rd Int. Conf. on GeoSpatial Semantics*, pages 140–158, 2009. DOI: 10.1007/978-3-642-10436-7_9 Cited on page(s) 27

P. Jain, P. Hitzler, A. Sheth, K. Verma, and P. Yeh. Ontology alignment for linked open data. In *Proc. 9th Int. Semantic Web Conf.*, pages 402–417, 2010. DOI: 10.1007/978-3-642-17746-0_26 Cited on page(s) 27

P. Jain, P. Yeh, K. Verma, R. Vasquez, M. Damova, P. Hitzler, and A. Sheth. Contextual ontology alignment of LOD with an upper ontology: A case study with proton. In *Proc. 8th Extended Semantic Web Conf.*, pages 80–92, 2011. DOI: 10.1007/978-3-642-21034-1_6 Cited on page(s) 27

R. Jain. Eventweb: Developing a human-centered computing system. *Comput.*, 41(2):42–50, 2008. DOI: 10.1109/MC.2008.49 Cited on page(s) 96, 97

B. Jansen, D. Booth, and A. Spink. Determining the informational, navigational, and transactional intent of web queries. *Information Proc. & Man.*, 44(3):1251–1266, 2008. DOI: 10.1016/j.ipm.2007.07.015 Cited on page(s) 17

D. Jones, T. Bench-Capon, and P. Visser. Methodologies for ontology development. In *Proc. IT&KNOWS Conference of the 15th IFIP World Computer Congress*, pages 20–35, 1998. Cited on page(s) 31

V. Kashyap and A. Sheth. Semantics-based information brokering. In *Proc. 3rd Int. Conf. on Information and Knowledge Management*, pages 363–370, 1994. DOI: 10.1145/191246.191309 Cited on page(s) 16

V. Kashyap, C. Ramakrishnan, C. Thomas, and A. Sheth. TaxaMiner: An experimentation framework for automated taxonomy bootstrapping. *Int. J. of Web and Grid Services*, 1(2):240–266, 2005. DOI: 10.1504/IJWGS.2005.008322 Cited on page(s) 18

M. Kifer and V. Subrahmanian. Theory of generalized annotated logic programming and its applications. *J. Logic Programming*, 12(4):335–367, 1992. DOI: 10.1016/0743-1066(92)90007-P Cited on page(s) 15

W. E. A. Klas and A. Sheth. *Multimedia Data Management: Using Metadata to Integrated and Apply Digital Data*. Springer Verlag, 1998. Cited on page(s) 35, 50

J. Kleinberg. Authoritative sources in a hyperlinked environment. *J. ACM*, 46(5):604–632, 1999. DOI: 10.1145/324133.324140 Cited on page(s) 17

D. Koller, A. Levy, and A. Pfeffer. P-classic: A tractable probabilistic description logic. In *Proc. 14th National Conf. on Artificial Intelligence and 9th Innovative Applications of Artificial Intelligence Conf.*, pages 390–397, 1997. Cited on page(s) 15

J. Kopecky, T. Vitvar, C. Bournez, and J. Farrell. Sawsdl: Semantic annotations for wsdl and xml schema. *IEEE Internet Comput.*, 11(6):60–67, 2007. DOI: 10.1109/MIC.2007.134 Cited on page(s) 70

J. Kopecky, K. Gomadam, and T. Vitvar. HRESTS: An HTML microformat for describing REST-ful web services. In *Proc. IEEE/WIC/ACM Int. Conf. on Web Intelligence and Intelligent Agent Technology*, pages 619–625, 2008. DOI: 10.1109/WIIAT.2008.379 Cited on page(s) 46

L. Lakshmanan and K. Thirunarayan. Declarative frameworks for inheritance. In Jan Chomicki and Gunter Saake, editors, *Logics for Databases and Information Systems*, pages 357–388. Kluwer Academic Publishers, 1998. DOI: 10.1007/978-1-4615-5643-5 Cited on page(s) 26

R. Lara, I. Cantador, and P. Castells. Semantic web technologies for the financial domain. In Jorge Cardoso, Martin Hepp, and Miltiadis D. Lytras, editors, *The Semantic Web: Real-World Applications from Industry*, number 6 in Semantic Web And Beyond Computing for Human Experience, pages 41–74. 2007. Cited on page(s) 62

L. Larkey and W. Croft. Combining classifiers in text categorization. In *Proc. 19th Annual Int. ACM SIGIR Conf. on Research and Development in Information Retrieval*, pages 289–297, 1996. DOI: 10.1145/243199.243276 Cited on page(s) 55

J. Lathem, K. Gomadam, and A. Sheth. SA-REST and (s) mashups: Adding semantics to RESTful services. *Proc. 1st IEEE Int. Conf. on Semantic Computing*, pages 469–476, 2007. DOI: 10.1109/ICSC.2007.79 Cited on page(s) 78, 81

L. Lefort, C. Henson, and K. Taylor. Semantic sensor network XG final report. W3C Incubator Group Report, 2011. URL http://www.w3.org/2005/Incubator/ssn/XGR-ssn-20110628/. Cited on page(s) 90

Y. Li and A. Jain. Classification of text documents. *Comp. J.*, 41(8):537–546, 1998. Cited on page(s) 55

R. Liere and P. Tadepalli. Active learning with committees for text categorization. In *Proc. 14th National Conf. on Artificial Intelligence and 9th Innovative Applications of Artificial Intelligence Conf.*, pages 591–597, 1997. Cited on page(s) 55

T. Lukasiewicz. Weak nonmonotonic probabilistic logics. *Artificial Intelligence*, 168(1):119–161, 2005. DOI: 10.1016/j.artint.2005.05.005 Cited on page(s) 15

A. Manjunatha, P. Anderson, A. Ranabahu, and A. Sheth. Identifying and implementing the underlying operators for nuclear magnetic resonance based metabolomics data analysis. In *Proc. 3rd Int. Conf. on Bioinformatics and Computational Biology*, pages 205–209, 2011. Cited on page(s) 124, 125

C. Manning, P. Raghavan, and H. Schutze. *Introduction to Information Retrieval*, volume 1. Cambridge University Press, 2008. DOI: 10.1017/CBO9780511809071 Cited on page(s) 11, 13, 17

D. Martin and J. Domingue. Semantic web services, part 1. *IEEE Intelligent Systems*, 22(5):12–17, 2007a. DOI: 10.1109/MIS.2007.94 Cited on page(s) 81

D. Martin and J. Domingue. Semantic web services, part 2. *IEEE Intelligent Systems*, 22(6):8–15, 2007b. DOI: 10.1109/MIS.2007.118 Cited on page(s) 81

D. Martin, M. Burstein, J. Hobbs, O. Lassila, D. McDermott, S. McIlraith, S. Narayanan, M. Paolucci, B. Parsia, T. Payne, E. Sirin, N. Srinivasan, and K. Sycara. OWL-S: Semantic markup for web services. W3C Member submission, 2004. URL `http://www.w3.org/Submission/OWL-S/`. Cited on page(s) 70

P. Mendes, P. Kapanipathi, and A. Passant. Twarql: Tapping into the wisdom of the crowd. In *Proc. 6th Int. Conf. on Semantic Systems*, pages 1–3, 2010. DOI: 10.1145/1839707.1839762 Cited on page(s) 110, 136, 137

B. Meyer. *Object-Oriented Software Construction*, volume 2. Prentice Hall, 1997. Cited on page(s) 32

P. Mika. *Social Networks and the Semantic Web (Semantic Web and Beyond*. Springer, 2007. Cited on page(s) 106

U. Miller. Thesaurus construction: problems and their roots. *Information Proc. & Man.*, 33:481–493, 1997. DOI: 10.1016/S0306-4573(97)00009-5 Cited on page(s) 23

T. Mitchell, J. Betteridge, A. Carlson, E. Hruschka, and R. Wang. Populating the semantic web by macro-reading internet text. *Proc. 8th Int. Semantic Web Conf.*, pages 998–1002, 2009. DOI: 10.1007/978-3-642-04930-9_66 Cited on page(s) 26

D. Nadeau and S. Sekine. A survey of named entity recognition and classification. *Lingvisticae Investigationes*, 30(1):3–26, 2007. DOI: 10.1075/li.30.1.03nad Cited on page(s) 101

M. Nagarajan, K. Verma, A. Sheth, J. Miller, and J. Lathem. Semantic interoperability of web services – challenges and experiences. *Proc. IEEE Int. Conf. on Web Services*, pages 373–382, 2006. DOI: 10.1109/ICWS.2006.116 Cited on page(s) 68, 74, 122

M. Nagarajan, K. Baid, A. Sheth, and S. Wang. Monetizing user activity on social networks - challenges and experiences. In *Proc. 2009 IEEE/WIC/ACM Int. Conf. on Web Intelligence and Intelligent Agent Technology*, pages 92–99, 2009a. DOI: 10.1109/WI-IAT.2009.20 Cited on page(s) 103

M. Nagarajan, K. Gomadam, A. Sheth, A. Ranabahu, R. Mutharaju, and A. Jadhav. Spatio-temporal-thematic analysis of citizen sensor data – challenges and experiences. In *Proc. 10th Int. Conf. on Web Information Systems Eng.*, pages 539–553, 2009b. DOI: 10.1007/978-3-642-04409-0_52 Cited on page(s) 109, 133, 136

E. Neumann. Finding the critical path: applying the semantic web to drug discovery and development. *Drug Discovery World*, 6(4):25–33, 2005. Cited on page(s) 62

E. K. Neumann and D. Quan. BioDASH: A semantic web dashboard for drug development. In *Proc. Pacific Symp. on Biocomputing*, pages 176–187, 2006. Cited on page(s) 62

Nokia. Sensing the world with mobile devices. Nokia Technology Insights Series, Nokia Research Center (NRC), 2008. URL `http://research.nokia.com/files/insight/NTI_Sensing_-_Dec_2008.pdf`. Cited on page(s) 2, 83

N.F. Noy and D.L. McGuinness. Ontology development 101: A guide to creating your first ontology. Technical Report KSL-01-05, Stanford University Knowledge Systems Laboratory, 2001. Cited on page(s) 29, 30, 31, 32

L. Obrst. Ontologies for semantically interoperable systems. In *Proc. 12th Int. Conf. on Information and Knowledge Management*, pages 366–369, 2003. DOI: 10.1145/956863.956932 Cited on page(s) 33

N. Oldham. Semantic ws-agreement partner selection. Master's thesis, University of Georgia, 2006. URL `http://athenaeum.libs.uga.edu/handle/10724/8901`. Cited on page(s) 68

T. OReilly. What is web 2.0: Design patterns and business models for the next generation of software. *Communications & Strategies*, (1):17, 2007. Cited on page(s) 5

R. Pan, Z. Ding, Y. Yu, and Y. Peng. A Bayesian network approach to ontology mapping. In *Proc. 4th Int. Semantic Web Conf.*, pages 563–577, 2005. DOI: 10.1007/11574620_41 Cited on page(s) 15

C. Pedrinaci, J. Domingue, and A. Sheth. Semantic web services. In *Handbook of Semantic Web Technologies*, volume 2, pages 977–1035. Springer, 2011. DOI: 10.1007/978-3-540-92913-0_22 Cited on page(s) 65, 69, 78, 79

I. Peters. *Folksonomies: Indexing and Retrieval in Web 2.0*. de Gruyter, 2009. DOI: 10.1515/9783598441851 Cited on page(s) 25

D. L. Phuoc, H. N. M. Quoc, J. X. Parreira, and M. Hauswirth. The linked sensor middleware – connecting the real world and the semantic web. In *Proc. 10th Int. Semantic Web Conf.*, 2011. Cited on page(s) 83

D. A. Plaisted. Equational reasoning and term rewriting systems. In D. M. Gabbay, C. J. Hogger, and J. A. Robinson, editors, *Handbook of Logic in Artificial Intelligence and Logic Programming*, volume 1: Logical Foundations, pages 273–364. Clarendon Press, 1993. Cited on page(s) 26

M. Plusch and C. Fry. *Water: Simplified Web Services and XML Programming*. Wiley, 2003. Cited on page(s) 23

J. Pschorr, C. Henson, H. Patni, and A. Sheth. Sensor discovery on linked data. Technical report, Kno.e.sis Center, Wright University, 2010. URL `http://knoesis.wright.edu/library/download/eswc2010sensornetworkstrack.pdf`. Cited on page(s) 97

R. Ramakrishnan and J. Gehrke. *Database management systems.* McGraw Hill, 2002. Cited on page(s) 18

A. Ranabahu, A. Sheth, A. Manjunatha, and K. Thirunarayan. Towards cloud mobile hybrid application generation using semantically enriched domain specific languages. In *Proc. Int. Workshop on Mobile Computing and Clouds*, 2010. DOI: 10.1007/978-3-642-29336-8_24 Cited on page(s) 134

A. Ranabahu, P. Parikh, M. Panahiazar, A. Sheth, and F. Logan-Klumpler. Kino: A generic document management system for biologists using SA-REST and faceted search. In *Proc. 5th IEEE Int. Conf. on Semantic Computing*, pages 205–208, 2011a. DOI: 10.1109/ICSC.2011.79 Cited on page(s) 81, 82

A. H. Ranabahu. *An Abstraction Driven Methodology for Application and Data Portability in Cloud Computing.* PhD thesis, Wright State University, 2012. Cited on page(s) 119

A. H. Ranabahu, E. M. Maximilien, A. P. Sheth, and K. Thirunarayan. A domain specific language for enterprise grade cloud-mobile hybrid applications. In *Proc. 11th Workshop on Domain-Specific Modeling*, pages 77–84, 2011b. DOI: 10.1145/2095050.2095064 Cited on page(s) 123, 124, 134

D. Reynolds. Amateur introduction to description logics. Technical report, Hewlett-Packard Laboratory, 2001. URL `http://www.hpl.hp.com/semweb/download/DescriptionLogicsIntro.pdf`. Cited on page(s) 6

S. Sahoo. *Semantic Provenance: Modeling, Querying, and Application in Scientific Discovery.* PhD thesis, Wright State University, 2010. Cited on page(s) 56

S Sahoo, A. Sheth, and C. Henson. Semantic provenance for escience: Managing the deluge of scientific data. *IEEE Internet Comput.*, 12(4):46–54, 2008. DOI: 10.1109/MIC.2008.86 Cited on page(s) 56

E. Sanchez. *Fuzzy Logic and the Semantic Web.* Elsevier, 2006. Cited on page(s) 11

F. Sebastiani. Machine learning in automated text categorization. *ACM Comput. Surv.*, 34(1):1–47, 2002. DOI: 10.1145/505282.505283 Cited on page(s) 55

A. Sheth. Computing for human experience. URL `http://knoesis.org/index.php/Computing_For_Human_Experience`. DOI: 10.1109/ICSMC.1988.754390 Cited on page(s) 139

A. Sheth. Semantic meta data for enterprise information integration. *DM Review*, 13(7):52–53, 2003. DOI: 10.1109/SECON.2007.342892 Cited on page(s) 51, 69

A. Sheth. Enterprise applications of semantic web: The sweet spot of risk and compliance. In *Proc. 1st Int. IFIP/WG12.5 Working Conf. on Industrial Applications of Semantic Web*, pages 47–62, 2005. Cited on page(s) 62

A. Sheth. Semantic web applications in financial industry, government, health care and life sciences. Keynote Talk at: AAAI Spring Symposium Semantic Web Meets eGovenment, 2006. URL `http://knoesis.org/library/resource.php?id=00037`. Cited on page(s) 62

A. Sheth. Citizen sensing, social signals, and enriching human experience. *IEEE Internet Computing*, 13(4):80–85, 2009. DOI: 10.1109/MIC.2009.77 Cited on page(s) 101, 102

A. Sheth. Computing for human experience: Semantics-empowered sensors, services, and social computing on the ubiquitous web. *IEEE Internet Comput.*, 14(1):88–91, 2010. DOI: 10.1109/MIC.2010.4 Cited on page(s) 8, 127, 139, 140

A. Sheth and M. Nagarajan. Semantics-empowered social computing. *IEEE Internet Comput.*, 13 (1):76–80, 2009. DOI: 10.1109/MIC.2009.21 Cited on page(s) 104, 105, 107

A. Sheth and M. Perry. Traveling the semantic web through space, time, and theme. *IEEE Internet Comput.*, 12(2):81–86, 2008. DOI: 10.1109/MIC.2008.46 Cited on page(s) 84, 97

A. Sheth and A. Ranabahu. Semantic modeling for cloud computing, part 1. *IEEE Internet Comput.*, 14(3):81–83, 2010a. DOI: 10.1109/MIC.2010.77 Cited on page(s) 115, 116

A. Sheth and A. Ranabahu. Semantic modeling for cloud computing, part 2. *IEEE Internet Comput.*, 14(4):81–84, 2010b. DOI: 10.1109/MIC.2010.98 Cited on page(s) 115, 118, 121, 123

A. Sheth, D. Avant, and C. Bertram. System and method for creating a semantic web and its applications in browsing, searching, profiling, personalization and advertising. US Patent 6,311,194, 2001. Cited on page(s) 17, 54

A. Sheth, C. Bertram, D. Avant, B. Hammond, K. Kochut, and Y. Warke. Managing semantic content for the web. *IEEE Internet Comput.*, 6(4):80–87, 2002. DOI: 10.1109/MIC.2002.1020330 Cited on page(s) 13, 17, 54, 58, 62, 113

A. Sheth, I. Arpinar, and V. Kashyap. Relationships at the heart of semantic web: Modeling, discovering, and exploiting complex semantic relationships. In Masoud Nikravesh, Ben Azvine, Ronald Yager, and Lotfi A. Zadeh, editors, *Enhancing the Power of the Internet*, volume 139 of *Studies in Fuzziness and Soft Computing*, pages 63–94. Springer, 2004. Cited on page(s) 5, 7, 38

154 BIBLIOGRAPHY

A. Sheth, B. Aleman-Meza, I. Arpinar, C. Bertram, Y. Warke, C. Ramakrishanan, C. Halaschek, K. Anyanwu, D. Avant, F. Arpinar, and et al. Semantic association identification and knowledge discovery for national security applications. *J. Database Manage.*, 16(1):33–53, 2005a. Cited on page(s) 62

A. Sheth, C. Ramakrishnan, and C. Thomas. Semantics for the semantic web: the implicit, the formal and the powerful. *J. Semantic Web and Information Systems*, 1:1–18, 2005b. Cited on page(s) 11

A. Sheth, S. Agrawal, J. Lathem, N. Oldham, H. Wingate, P. Yadav, and K. Gallagher. Active semantic electronic medical record. In *Proc. 5th Int. Semantic Web Conf.*, pages 913–926, 2006a. DOI: 10.1007/11926078_66 Cited on page(s) 62

A. Sheth, K. Verma, and K. Gomadam. Semantics to energize the full services spectrum. *Commun. ACM*, 49(7):55–61, 2006b. DOI: 10.1145/1139949 Cited on page(s) 67

A. Sheth, K. Gomadam, and A. Ranabahu. Semantics enhanced services: Meteor-S, SAWSDL and SA-REST. *Q. Bull. IEEE TC on Data Eng.*, 31(3):8–12, 2008a. Cited on page(s) 70

A. Sheth, C. Henson, and S. Sahoo. Semantic sensor web. *IEEE Internet Comput.*, 12(4):78–83, 2008b. DOI: 10.1109/MIC.2008.87 Cited on page(s) 83, 85, 89, 93, 134, 137

A. Sheth, C. Thomas, and P. Mehra. Continuous semantics to analyze real-time data. *IEEE Internet Comput.*, 14(6):84–89, 2010. DOI: 10.1109/MIC.2010.137 Cited on page(s) 110, 135, 136, 137, 140

A. P. Sheth and S. Stephens. Semantic web: Technologies and applications for the real-world. In *Proc. 16th Int. World Wide Web Conf.*, pages 8–12, 2007. Cited on page(s) 62

Amit Sheth. Changing focus on interoperability in information systems: From system, syntax, structure to semantics. In *Interoperating Geographic Information Systems*, pages 5–30. Kluwer Academic Publishers, 1998. Cited on page(s) 49

P. Sheth, K. Gomadam, and J. Lathem. SA-REST: Semantically interoperable and easier-to-use services and mashups. *IEEE Internet Comput.*, 11(6):91–94, 2007. DOI: 10.1109/MIC.2007.133 Cited on page(s) 70, 80, 122

O. Shilovitsky. Friday data stories: Linked enterprise data. Nokia Technology Insights Series, 2011. URL http://research.nokia.com/files/insight/NTI_Sensing_-_Dec_2008.pdf. Cited on page(s) 55

Y. L. Simmhan, B. Plale, and D. Gannon. A survey of data provenance in e-science. *ACM SIGMOD Rec.*, 34:31–36, 2005. DOI: 10.1145/1084805.1084812 Cited on page(s) 57

K. Sivashanmugam, K. Verma, A. Sheth, and J. Miller. Adding semantics to web services standards. In *Proc. IEEE Int. Conf. on Web Services*, pages 395–401, 2003. Cited on page(s) 70, 117

R. Stevens, J. Zhao, and C. Goble. Using provenance to manage knowledge of in silico experiments. *Brief. Bioinform.*, 8(3):183–194, 2007. DOI: 10.1093/bib/bbm015 Cited on page(s) 57

U. Straccia. A fuzzy description logic. In *Proc. 15th National Conf. on Artificial Intelligence and 10th Innovative Applications of Artificial Intelligence Conf.*, pages 594–599, 1998. Cited on page(s) 15

U. Straccia. Uncertainty and description logic programs: A proposal for expressing rules and uncertainty on top of ontologies. Technical Report Technical Report 2004-TR-14, ISTI-CNR, 2004. URL http://nmis.isti.cnr.it/~straccia/projects/Material/Papers/TR-UDLLPSemWeb/TR-UDLLPSemWeb.pdf. Cited on page(s) 15

W.C. Tan. Provenance in databases: Past, current, and future. *Q. Bull. IEEE TC on Data Eng.*, 30 (4):3–12, 2007. Cited on page(s) 57

K. Thirunarayan. Local theories of inheritance. *Int. J. Intelligent Syst.*, 10:617–645, 1995. Cited on page(s) 22

K. Thirunarayan. On embedding machine-processable semantics into documents. *IEEE Trans. Knowl. and Data Eng.*, 17:1014–1018, 2005. Cited on page(s) 23, 55, 59

K. Thirunarayan and T. Immaneni. Integrated retrieval from web of documents and data. In Zbigniew Ras and Agnieszka Dardzinska, editors, *Advances in Data Management*, volume 223 of *Studies in Computational Intelligence*, pages 25–48. Springer, 2009. Cited on page(s) 16

K. Thirunarayan and M. Kifer. A theory of nonmonotonic inheritance based on annotated logic. *Artificial Intelligence*, 60(1):23–50, 1993. Cited on page(s) 15, 22

K. Thirunarayan and J. K. Pschorr. Semantic information and sensor networks. In *Proc. 2009 ACM Symp. on Applied Computing*, pages 1273–1274, 2009. Cited on page(s) 86, 87, 97

K. Thirunarayan, A. Berkovich, and D. Sokol. An information extraction approach to reorganizing and summarizing specifications. *Inf. and Softw. Tech.*, 47(4):215–232, 2005. Cited on page(s) 23, 59

C. Thomas, P. Mehra, R. Brooks, and A. Sheth. Growing fields of interest-using an expand and reduce strategy for domain model extraction. In *Proc. 2008 IEEE/WIC/ACM Int. Conf. on Web Intelligence and Intelligent Agent Technology*, volume 1, pages 496–502, 2008. Cited on page(s) 117, 135

C. J. Thomas. Knowledge acquisition from community-generated content, 2011. URL http://www.knoesis.org/research/semweb/projects/knowledge-extraction. Cited on page(s) 25

S. Tobies. Complexity results and practical algorithms for logics in knowledge representation. arXiv preprint cs/0106031, 2001. Cited on page(s) 21

D. S. Touretzky, J. F. Horty, and R. H. Thomas. A clash of intuitions: The current state of non-monotonic multiple inheritance systems. In *Proc. 10th Int. Joint Conf. on AI*, pages 476–482, 1987. Cited on page(s) 22

V. Uren, P. Cimiano, J. Iria, S. Handschuh, M. Vargas-Vera, E. Motta, and F. Ciravegna. Semantic annotation for knowledge management: Requirements and a survey of the state of the art. *J. Web Semantics*, 4(1):14–28, 2006. Cited on page(s) 35

M. Uschold. Where are the semantics in the semantic web? *AI Magazine*, 24(3):25–36, 2003. Cited on page(s) 11

M. Uschold and M. Gruninger. Ontologies: Principles, methods and applications. *The Knowledge Engineering Review*, 11(2):93–136, 1996. Cited on page(s) 30

W. van Der Aalst, A. TerHofstede, B. Kiepuszewski, and A. Barros. Workflow patterns. *Distrib. Parall. Databases*, 14(1):5–51, 2003. Cited on page(s) 71

K. Verma. *Configuration and Adaptation of Semantic Web Processes*. PhD thesis, University of Georgia, 2006. URL http://athenaeum.libs.uga.edu/handle/10724/9083. Cited on page(s) 68, 73, 78

K. Verma, K. Sivashanmugam, A. Sheth, A. Patil, S. Oundhakar, and J. Miller. Meteor-S WSDI: A scalable P2P infrastructure of registries for semantic publication and discovery of web services. *Inf. Tech. & Man.*, 6(1):17–39, 2005. Cited on page(s) 68, 73

M Weiser. The computer for the 21st century. *Scientific American*, 265(3):66–75, September 1991. Cited on page(s) 139

K. Whitehouse, F. Zhao, and J. Liu. Semantic streams: A framework for composable semantic interpretation of sensor data. In *Proc. 3rd European Workshop on Wireless Sensor Networks*, pages 5–20, 2006. Cited on page(s) 138

Wikipedia. Computational linguistics, 2011. URL http://en.wikipedia.org/wiki/Computational_linguistics. Cited on page(s) 11

D. Wood. *Linking Enterprise Data*. Springer, 2010. Cited on page(s) 50, 55

W. A. Woods. Meaning and links: A semantic odyssey. In *Proc. 9th Int. Conf. Principles of Knowledge Representation and Reasoning*, pages 740–742, 2004. Cited on page(s) 12

B. Worthen. Mashups sew data together: Software tools can cut costs, time for linking information sources. The Wall Street J, July 2007. URL http://online.wsj.com/article/SB118584045835882843.html. Cited on page(s) 65

Yahoo. Hadoop tutorial, 2012. URL `http://developer.yahoo.com/hadoop/tutorial/module4.html`. Cited on page(s) 134

L. Zadeh. Toward a perception-based theory of probabilistic reasoning with imprecise probabilities. *J. Statistical Planning and Inference*, 105(1):233–264, 2002. Cited on page(s) 15

L.A. Zadeh. Inference in fuzzy logic via generalized constraint propagation. In *Proc. 26th Int. Symp. on Multiple-Valued Logic*, pages 192–195, 1996. Cited on page(s) 11, 14

L.A. Zadeh. From search engines to question-answering systems: The role of fuzzy logic. *Progress in Informatics*, 1:1–3, 2005. Cited on page(s) 12

I. Zuzak. Why understanding REST is hard and what we should do about it - systematization, models and terminology for REST, 2010. URL `http://ivanzuzak.info/2010/04/03/why-understanding-rest-is-hard-and-what-we-should-do-about-it-systematization-models-and-terminology-for-rest.html`. Cited on page(s) 45, 64

I. Zuzak, I. Budiselic, and G. Delac. A finite-state machine approach for modeling and analyzing restful systems. *J. Web Eng.*, 10(4):353–390, 2011. Cited on page(s) 64